Islands of Steel

The Viability of the Supercarrier in the 21st Century

Timothy Wayne Burford

"Whether or not we decide to remain shackled to the past will determine the fate not only of the United States ... but of the whole of humanity. The world is changing rapidly, and that is not necessarily bad. But change can be tough, and we need to deal with it."

- Naval Postgraduate School Commencement, Naval Post Graduate School, Monterey, CA, September 21, 2007.

Abstract

"It is the function of the Navy to carry the war to the enemy so that it is not fought on U.S. soil." – Chester W. Nimitz

The Supercarrier is the natural evolution in design from the *Essex* class fleet carriers that significantly contributed to the American victory over Japan in World War Two. These nuclear-powered symbols of national prestige and military might have been a fundamental element of United States foreign policy ever since, showing the flag, performing missions of mercy, providing demonstrations of martial resolve and projecting power into the farthest corners of the globe. However, much like the battleship before it, the Supercarrier is threatened by technological developments abroad and resource limitations at home. Emergent technologies such as the Anti-Ship Ballistic Missile, the Hypersonic Anti-Ship Cruise Missile and supercavitating torpedoes collude with the extreme cost of building and maintaining the vessels to force an evaluation of the vulnerability and value of the Supercarrier concept in future wars.

Islands of Steel provides a retrospective on the ascendancy of the aircraft carrier over the battleship as the primary capital ship, a brief combat history of the WWII American aircraft carrier as well as insight into the post-WWII experience of the nuclear Supercarrier including its significance to United States foreign policy. This book is intended to stimulate continued discussion into the viability of the Supercarrier concept in the emerging technological and geostrategic era, investigate nascent threats and countermeasure options regarding carrier task force defense as well as provide a prospectus of alternative concepts to the Supercarriers' costly investment requirement and continued deployment.

Table of Contents

Introduction

The United States Navy's nuclear-powered Supercarrier is the pinnacle of naval surface warship design. At once the ultimate manifestation of geostrategic hegemonic prestige and a decidedly effectual means of rapid and sustained power projection to every potential point of conflict on Earth, the Supercarriers unlimited range and persistent on-point duration provides the White House with a powerful diplomacy tool simply through its ominous presence - and the Pentagon with a flexible means of deploying forces to regions where ground-based options are limited. Expensive beyond the capacity of any other nation to build and maintain, the nuclear-powered Supercarrier is uniquely American and as history reveals has been a quintessential element in the global ascendancy of the United States since the Second World War.

However, like the battleship before it, the Supercarrier is threatened with obsolescence in a dynamic technical and strategic environment. Nascent threats are emerging that may render the Supercarrier vulnerable and therefore too financially - and collaterally – expensive to warrant further expenditure in an era of declining resources. This begs the question: Are American Supercarriers still a viable means of projecting influence and military power in the emergent geo-strategic and technological environment? The answer may well be that it is time to consider other options.

To put this question into perspective, a review of the historical circumstances and technological developments that led to the ascension of the carrier over the battleship and its later significance to American hegemony is obligatory for contextual purposes. We begin with an unlikely hero and brilliant geostrategic visionary: Alfred Thayer Mahan.

Alfred Thayer Mahan: Architect of American Global Supremacy

From its humble origins as one of many 18th Century British colonies, the United States of America emerged in the 21st Century as *the* global hegemon and ultimately the sole surviving Superpower of the Post-WWII Era, having long ago eclipsed its martial mentor England as the supreme military, diplomatic and socio-economic influence on the planet. The United States owes much of this unlikely and relatively meteoric ascension to planetary dominance to an equally unlikely champion; a seasick-prone, navigationally challenged nautical Luddite named Alfred Thayer Mahan. More at home in academia than on the high seas, Alfred Thayer Mahan nonetheless generated maritime-based geostrategic theories that were instrumental to the ascension of the United States to global dominance during the 20th Century.

The son of famed West Point military engineering professor Dennis Hart Mahan, whose teaching influenced United States Military Academy graduates serving on both sides during the American Civil War, Alfred Thayer Mahan was born at West Point, New York, September 27, 1840, his middle name his father's tribute to Colonel Sylvanus Thayer, West Point's second and most influential superintendent. Though stemming from such a West Point background focus, Alfred Thayer Mahan – against his father's will - graduated from the United States Naval Academy at Annapolis in 1859 as second in his class.[1] Mahan served aboard several vessels during the American Civil War, seeing notable action at the Battle of Port Royal on November 7, 1861. Remaining in the United States Navy in the decades following the war and serving aboard several vessels in various capacities, Mahan would eventually be promoted to captain in 1885.

---

[1] Trevor Dupuy. *The Harper Encyclopedia of Military Biography.* Edison, NJ: Castle Books, 1992, 477-478.

As a commander of vessels Captain Mahan's performance was unremarkable, if at times fraught with difficulties, colliding with several objects and vessels in the course of his captaincy.[2] This navigational shortcoming, combined with his propensity for sea sickness and a love of academia, led Mahan to duties ashore, where he served ultimately as President of the Naval War College, lecturing on naval tactics and geostrategic theory beginning in 1886.[3] It was during this period that Mahan undertook an in-depth study of the influence of the Royal Navy on the expansion and maintenance of the British Empire. These studies led to his conclusion that the Royal Navy was quintessential to the British Empire's establishment and continued existence as a martial and commercial global power, and from these studies, Mahan distilled a theoretical construct that would ultimately allow the United States to emulate this achievement. How the

[2] Peter Paret *The Makers of Modern Strategy from Machiavelli to the Nuclear Age*. Princeton, NJ: Princeton University Press, 1986, 445.

[3] Allan R. Millet, Peter Maslowski, and William Feis. *For the Common Defense*. New York: Free Press, 2012, 245-246.

British Isles, a relatively minute geographical feature on the
planetary surface, came to dominate the planet in the 17th and
18th Centuries, was a subject of much interest to Mahan, who
by 1890 had congealed his insights into a published and
influential body of work entitled *The Influence of Sea Power
on History 1660-1783*. In this, his first of several works,
Mahan denotes the importance of the lessons of history on
contemporary and future strategists, concentrating, as one
might expect, on the influence of sea-power on warfare and
nation building in Europe.[4]

Mahan notes, for instance, in his introduction to *The
Influence of Sea Power*, that historians of his age tended to
overlook the importance of mastery of the sea in the outcome
of historical campaigns. Scipio Africanus' victory against
Hannible at Zama and Wellington's against Napoleon at
Waterloo, Mahan points out, were ultimately executed far

---

[4] Alfred Thayer Mahan. "The Influence of Sea Power on History
1660-1783." *The Project Gutenberg.* September 26, 1890/2004.
http://www.gutenberg.org/files/13529/13529-h/13529-h.htm
(accessed December 29, 2016).

from the victor's shores, meaning that master of the sea was essential to their ultimate outcomes.[5] The campaigns of Alexander and a later Richard Lion Heart in the Middle East, too, one could argue, could be presented as examples of sea-power assisted operations that historians had often abridged to land battles. At the same time Mahan lamented the isolated perspective of British naval historians of his time, serving, in his view, as chronicalers of singular events rather than seeing said events as intrical pieces in the mosaicof military history. Command of the sea, Mahan argued, was elemental to victory on land, particularly in the case of oceanic powers such as Britain and, ultimately, the United States.

From this foundation, Mahan pursues the notion that sea power must be studied as elemental to military history in general and not as a separate part. This notion is reinforced by the realization that the fate of Europe lay at one time in the hands of the Vikings, whose naval capacity afforded them the ability to launch amphibious assaults on unsuspecting targets

[5] Ibid.

far ranging from their homelands. To this end, Mahan views

the oceans as a "great highway", a "wide common" upon

which the fate of nations are forged and maintained.[6] He

viewed maritime investment, both commercial and martial, as

essential to any seafaring nation or nation that otherwise

borders a sea. In the case of the British (and French) Empire,

these trade routes were the interconnective network through

which the nation's wealth and influence travelled, with their

protection by armed vessels essential to the colonial empire's

survival. Mahan, in his lengthy work, saw the wealth of the

British Empire in particular to stem from three elements:

Production of goods, shipping, and the network of colonies

that presented or accepted these goods. The Royal Navy,

charged with the protection of these elements, was primary to

the continuation of said global enterprise. Further, Mahan

noted, the capacity to "show the flag" and therefore provide a

global presence was equally essential to this construct: It gave

the nation in question the impression of ubiquity, particularly

---

[6] Ibid.

in the minds of lesser states, but also in the minds of peer
states, whose capacity to colonize was limited by the presence
of the Royal Navy.

In presenting his findings as important to the
emergence of the United States as a global power, Mahan, in
his later 1897 work, *The Interest of America in Sea Power,
Present and Future*, saw the need for the developing
manufacturing capacity of the United States to find a global
market for their goods. Domestic consumption of domestic
production was not ultimately profitable: foreign markets
were required to bring income into the country. Trade, in
short, was key to the development of a national identity of the
likes of the British Empire. This, as Mahan noted, would
require not only a production base, which was then being
increasing exponentially domestically in the United States,
but a shipping network and an overseas market, all dependent
on the establishment and maintenance of a relevant naval
force. This force, as Mahan envisioned, would, like the Royal
Navy before them, not only protect the sea lanes from piracy

and other-state influences, but provide a global presence that increases the diplomatic and commercial influence of the emergent power. As Mahan notes, "Control of a maritime region is insured primarily by a navy; secondarily, by positions, suitably chosen and spaced one from the other, upon which as bases the navy rests, and from which it can exert its strength."[7] Mahan concludes the first portion of this work by calling for an alliance with America's former rival, Britain, given their common needs in the coming era.

It is the potential for the rise of the United States to peer status with Britain that inspires Mahan's additional influential works, including *Armaments and Arbitration; Or the Place of Force in the International Relations of States*, in which he proposes the fortification of American interests abroad and the increased expenditure on naval power and overseas bases as an investment in national sovereignty.[8]

---

[7] Alfred Thayer Mahan. "The Interest of America in Sea Power, Present and Future." *The Project Gutenberg.* May 2, 1897/2005. http://www.gutenberg.org/files/15749/15749-h/15749-h.htm (accessed December 18, 2016).

[8] Mahan, Alfred Thayer. "Armaments and Arbitration; Or the Place

Mahan's clear desire was for the United States to usurp the British and French as a dominant world power, realizing the incredible capacity of the relatively new nation, now continentaly conplete after the Indian Wars, in resources and emergent production capacity at the dawn of the industrial age. Mahan, in short, saw the world as America's oyster.

Mahan's philosophy was not, however, salient in his time, but rather a distillation of naval thinking among top United States Navy officials, including then Secretary of the Navy Benjamin Tracy, who construed the "sea [as] the future seat of empire. And [the United States would] rule it as certainly as the sun doth rise!"[9] In fact, in the aftermath of the Indian Wars that completed America's Manifest Desitny ofWestward Expansion, American aspirations began to reach beyond the continental geography, in contrast to the isolationist leanings of the Founders, with an increased

of Force in the International Relations of States." *Archive.org.* 1912. https://archive.org/stream/cu31924007373560/cu31924007373560_ djvu.txt (accessed December 29, 2016).

[9] Millet, et al, *For the Common Defense*, 259.

realization for the need for a prominent naval force making its way into American martial planning. In fact, through the auspices of the earlier Monroe Doctrine, which addressed the possibility of European colonial re-expansionism into the Western Hemesphere, a "New American Imperialism" developed which would eventually lead to the Spanish-American War, the outcome of which was dependant upon American naval capacity both in its battle-fleet and its capacity to project and support land forces to remote regions such as Cuba and the Phillipines.[10]

Theodore Roosevelt's corollary to the Monroe Doctrine increased the latitude of the United States to respondmilitarily to European threats beyond those envisioned by Monroe, rendering the United States as an "international police power" in response to any perception of aggression against American interests in the Western Hemisphere.[11] Roosevelt's "Big Stick" gunboat diplomacy

---

[10] Eugene Jarecki. *The American Way of War.* New York: Free Press, 2008, 29.

was characterized by this projection capacity of naval force in the hands of the emergent American power. This increased global presence allowed for the "Dollar Diplomacy" of his successors, whereby American wealth and production capacity further enriched the nation at the expense of the embattled colonial powers of France and England during the early stages of the First World War.[12]

It was, in fact, Woodrow Wilson's involvement of the United States in the First World War and his subsequent Fourteen Points initiative, proposed at Versailles, that set the precedent for an end to American isolationism. And though America would return to an isolationist stance in the Post-WWI Era, events set in motion at Versailles and later with the onset of the Great Depression soon proved the United States to be intrinsically entangled in world affairs at the commercial, diplomatic, and ultimately martial level, a reality that informed Franklin Delano Roosevelt's foreign policy in

[11] Ibid.

[12] Jarecki, 30.

the years leading to the Second World War. In fact, it was under FDR that Mahan's theories truly came into their own, providing a foundation for American hegemony in the Post-WWII Era.

To provide a backdrop for the developments of the FDR period, one must return to Versailles, the 1919 treaty meant as a capstone to 'The War to End All Wars' that instead proved to be the impetus for the major conflicts that were to follow. Though many historians have noted the impact of Versailles (and the economic crisis of the Great Depression – viewed in Germany as symptomatic of globalist economics) on the rise of the Nazi party, few recall that the Japanese were also present at Versailles, proffering a racial equality addendum to the treaty that was rejected by the Europeans representatives.[13] This rejection would ultimately empower the militarists in Japan who believed that the nation would never get fair treatment in diplomatic negotiations with

---

[13] Charles Mee. *The End of Order: Versailles, 1919.* New York: Dutton, 1980, p 109.

the European powers. [Too, in a further historical connection, a Vietnamese nationalist named Nguyen Sinh Cung would make an attempt to plea to Wilson, a known anti-colonialist, for the end to European colonialism in Southeast Asia – a meeting avoided by Wilson for fear of alienating his French counterpart. This afront would force Cung into the arms of international socialism and the adaptation of a new moniker, Ho Chi Minh - and to the eventual involvement of the United States in one of its longest and costliest wars].[14]

By the mid-1930's, as America and the globe languished in the throes of the Great Depression, and as war clouds loomed in Europe and Asia, FDR, realizing the impending failure of his New Deal initiatives, sought to profit not only economically but strategically from the imminentglobal conflict. To this end, the president pursued a policy that would assure the eventual eruption of conflicts in these remote regions, with the goal of selling arms to Britain and France, thus profiting from the self-destruction of the

[14] Ibid, 110.

extent global hegemonic powers.[15] In Europe, though aware

of the plans of Colonel-General Ludwig Beck's *Schartz*

Kapelle (Black Orchestra) anti-Hitler group to arrest *der*

Fuhrer on the grounds of insanity if he actually invaded

Czechoslovakia should the British stand firm, withheld this

information from Neville Chamberlain prior to his meeting

with Hitler in Munich in 1936 – though he did supply it to

Churchill, who also withheld it from Chamberlain.[16] Beck's

group backed down after Chamberlain did because Hitler's

successful negotiations increased his popularity amongst

Germans. This Machiavellian maneuvering on FDR's part

was meant to insure the not only conflict in Europe but the

---

[15] Lynn Picknett, Stephan Prior, and Clive Prince. *Friendly Fire: The Secret War Between the Allies.* Edinburgh: Mainstream, 2005, p 116.

[16] Donald Watt. *Succeeding the Bull: America in Britain's place - A Study of the Anglo-American Relationship and World Politics in the Context of British and American Policy Making in the Twentieth Century.* Cambridge: Cambridge University Press, 1984, p 103-105; Klemmens von Klemperer. *German Resistance against Hitler: The Search for Aliies Abroad.* Oxford: Clarendon Press, 1992, 105-110; Lynn Picknett, Stephan Prior, and Clive Prince. *Friendly Fire: The Secret War Between the Allies.* Edinburgh: Mainstream, 2005, p 110-111; also Richard Lamb. *The Ghosts of Peace, 1935-1945.* Salsbury: Bloomsbury, 1987, p 70-73.

ascendancy of the American-friendly war hawk Winston

Churchill, both of which were necessary to an eventual arms

deal and the ultimate coup – the Bases for Destroyers Deal of

September 2, 1940, which provided the United States' with a

global network of naval bases that Mahan had deemed

necessary to global hegemony in exchange for fifty barely

operable and functionally obsolete WWI Era destroyers. With

the later signing of the Lend Lease Act on March 11, 1941

and the desperate British Government's need for material

support in the aftermath of the Battle for Britain, the

economic reliance and geostrategic usurping of the British

Empire by the United States was essentially complete.[17]

In Asia, Roosevelt's continued sanction of a militarily

expansive Japan, culminating in the oil embargo that would

ultimately drive Japan to military action to procure the

commodity, continued even when "Magic" revealed that the

---

[17] Donald Watt. *Succeeding the Bull: America in Britain's place - A Study of the Anglo-American Relationship and World Politics in the Context of British and American Policy Making in the Twentieth Century.* Cambridge: Cambridge University Press, 1984, p 103-105.

Japanese were readying for war and that an internal schism between political elements in Japan. Roosevelt cast off ambassadorial propositions in September of 1941 from peace-party Prime Minister Prince Konoe, who would resign in favor of the warmongering General Tojo. The latter immediately reject Roosevelt's counteroffer, made through Secretary of State Cordell Hull, to unfreeze Japanese assets and lift the oil embargo if Japan agreed to withdraw from the Asian mainland, recognized Chiang Kai-shek's nationalist government and retract from the Tripartite Pact with Germany and Italy.[18]

Doing so, of course, would make Japan reliant upon American imports and render it a *de facto* client state, as per Mahan, a culturally unacceptable condition for the Nipponese people as Roosevelt knew. Ergo, this demand, made on November 26, was intended to push the Japanese into a corner – a strategy meant to force the militarists in Japan into

---

[18] Lynn Picknett, Stephan Prior and Clive Prince. *Friendly Fire: The Secret War Between the Allies.* Edinburgh: Mainstream, 2005, p 242.

attacking British assets in the region, Roosevelt having

ordered the Pacific Fleet to move from the West Coast to

forward bases in Hawaii and the Philippines in the spring of

1941 to deter the Japanese from attacking American assets.

But instead, the November 26 demand elicited an

opposite and completely unintended response, his

Machiavellian maneuverings resulting in Japanese Admiral

Yamamoto's preemptive strike force sailing for Pearl Harbor

later that same day.[19] As noted by Peter Calvocoressi in *Total*

War: The Causes and Courses of the Second World War,

"Roosevelt steered [the US] resolutely on a course of

economic strangulation so intense and so aggressive that it

must result in war or the abject surrender of Japan to

America's implacable demands."[20] Though unaware of this

northerly force, Roosevelt *was* aware of *another* strike force

departing Japan in a southerly direction that same evening

---

[19] Ibid.

[20] Peter Calvocoressi. *Total War: The Causes and Courses of the Second World War.* London: Peguin, 1989, p 335.

toward the British naval base at Kota Bharu in northern Malaya, the US Navy shadowing them all the way from Japan, with timely information being forwarded to Washington, to the desk of FDR – who withheld this information from the British.[21]

Following the surprise attack on Pearl Harbor and the subsequent (and somewhat irrational) declaration of war on the United States by Hitler's Germany, the United States found itself embroiled in the very conflict that Roosevelt had hoped to avoid whilst profiting from – a metaphor of the potential consequences of playing with fire. However, this occurrence would provide the United States with a path toward global hegemony at an even more accelerated pace: The insulation of the seas and friendly adjoining states prevented the destruction of the American infrastructure during the course of the conflict, as it did to the major powers of Europe and Asia, whilst the Destroyer for Bases Deal

---

[21] Picknett et al, p 245-247; Aldrich, Richard. *Intelligence and the War against Japan.* Cambridge: Cambridge University Press, 2000, 49.

provided the Navy with forward projection power and presence and the Lend Lease Act (and the nature of the Pacific and Atlantic battlefields) provided funding and impetus for the expansion of the fleet.

And though many historians fail to point out the specific import, WWII was very much a marine war favoring the dominant sea powers in every theater of the conflict, with America in particular projecting its power by means of naval force and maritime assets be it in the more obvious Pacific or the less obvious arena of Europe where troops and material had to be transported to the fight in the first place. Though in despair of the entanglement beyond nationalistic profiteering, the bewilderment of technology and the grief of profound losses incurred during these events, Alfred Thayer Mahan would have been both awed and delighted at the execution of this geostrategic coup based upon his own theories. In a short period, the United States had usurped England and France as the West's preeminent power and provided itself, to a large degree, with the geostrategic tools necessary to deal with its next martial threat – global war with the Soviet Union.

Outwardly secure in its unilateral possession of the Atomic Bomb and weary of war, the United States disarmed in the months following WWII at a surprisingly rapid rate, as a domestic current of isolationism returned to the nation. However, with the fall of the Iron Curtain and the Soviet's rapid achievement of nuclear status, as well as the proxy entanglements in Korea and elsewhere, the need for a return to a status of engagement loomed large in the minds of American planners who now saw themselves living in an era of a potential nuclear Pearl Harbor.[22] This, in conjunction with the stated communist objective of global assimilation of their ideology by force if necessary, led the United States to a philosophy of aggressive containment of the Soviet Union as well as China. And though these powers maintained huge,

~~armored forces in Europe and~~ massive infantry forces in Asia,

[22] Newhouse, John. *War and Peace in the Nuclear Age*. New york: Knoff, 1989, 111.

the United States had one major advantage: The network of global bases acquired from England via FDR's Destroyers for Bases Deal and a large navy funded in part by the war debts of the former colonial powers that the United States was fundamental in rescuing from the advances of Nazi Germany.

In addition to the martial capacity of this basing network in containing and observing the opposition, the existence of these bases provided for a global presence of American diplomacy and culture, opening the door for commercial investment that further enhanced the comparative superiority of American ideology in the eyes of the Third World. This economic superiority, manifested in superior technology that eventually outstripped the Soviet capacity for continuing the ongoing arms race that constituted the Cold War, eventually led to its collapse in 1990 and the emergence of the United States as the sole surviving Superpower and *de facto* global hegemon in the waning days of the 20th Century.[23]

---

[23] USHistory.org. *End of the Cold War.* 2014. http://www.ushistory.org/us/59e.asp (accessed December 28, 2016).

In the immediate aftermath of the Cold War, the United States found itself confronted with a new set of geostrategic challenges, notably in the form of non-state actors, upstart nations and a re-emergent Russia and expansive China.[24] In the face of these new challenges, Mahan's theories have proven to hold true, the forward basing of American forces allowing for a forward power projection as well as a martial and diplomatic presence that ensures commercial opportunities in the farthest regions of the globe. As the future unfolds, the forward deployment of American assets such as Aegis Missile Cruisers and their network of bases may provide protection against nuclear missile assault by emergent rogue states while the existence of an advanced blue water navy ensures the safety of the American homeland from submarine-launched missiles and airborne assets.

Additionally, as the sole purveyor of Supercarrier technology, the United States Navy retains the capacity to

---

[24] Hal Brands. *From Berlin to Baghdad: America's Search for Purpose in the Post-Cold War Waorld.* Lexington: University of Kentucky Press, 2008, 122.

project its overwhelming power throughout the world, with their nuclear power allowing for a sustained and intimidating presence in problematic areas. This unique capacity, still unparalleled, gives the United States a powerful negotiating edge that has prevented open conflict at times and at others provided a strike capacity that does not require the use of bases in regions where political conditions are unfavorable to the launching of operations against specific targets.[25] The Supercarrier construct, with its extended reach and duration on point, provides the epitome of what Mahan had described in his influencial works, even if the author himself preferred the age of sail to the steel and steam vessels that were emergent in his time.

In the age of modernity, in an era of Russian and Chinese resurgence and a proliferation of non-state actors, the need for an expansive and capable naval force remains

---

[25] Momiyama, Thomas S. "Supercarriers for Smart Super Power Diplomacy." *Naval War College Review* (Naval War College) 63, no. 3 (June 2010): 168-174.

elemental to American foreign policy. Though still, at the time of this writing (2019), the dominant naval presence on the planet, the United States must look to the future, as Mahan did before, to address the impending threats to global hegemony that the nation at this point still enjoys. The reemergence of Russia and China as near-peer states, as well as the rise of regional powers such as Iran and North Korea, calls for the need for continued vigilance and preparation in the coming decades. Given the oceanic nature of the United States, bordered as it is on two sides by vast seas, the lessons garnered from Alfred Thayer Mahan's study of the Royal Navy and its import to the British Empire and how said lessons can benefit the United States remains applicable even in a world of supercarriers and nuclear submarines.

Alfred Thayer Mahan's prescience in his geostrategic thinking, a philosophy well founded in his historical studies of the importance of the Royal Navy to the creation and maintenance of the British Empire, has served his home nation well in the years following his writings, with martial planners in several nations, including Japan in the 1930s and '40s also benefitting from his insights. It was the United States, however, via the auspices of the Theodore Roosevelt, Woodrow Wilson, and Franklin Delano Roosevelt Administrations in particular, that benefitted most from his efforts. This paradigm would continue into the Cold War and beyond, providing the United States with the foundational element that has abetted its ascension to global dominance in the dawn of the 21st Century. Future planners would do well to keep Mahan's treatise in mind as America faces new challenges in the coming years.

Dreadnaught

1 HMS Dreadnaught (Public Domain).

For the first half of the twentieth century, the

dreadnaught battleship and its derivatives ruled the high seas.

These iron behemoths were the mechanical manifestations of

U.S. Navy Captain Alfred Thayer Mahan's theory of strategic

influence, formulated in his seminal work *The Influence of*

Sea Power on History, which has persuaded many nations'

naval theorists since 1890.[26] Mahan's contribution to military

and geo-political theory lay in his analysis of the significance

of the British Navy's oceanic dominance to the island nation's

---

[26] Allan R. Millett, Peter Maslowski, and William Feis. For the
Common Defense (New York: Free Press, 2012), 245-246.

global influence; a factor which he found to be fundamental. The reality that a prevailing naval presence had been primary to England's historic, if ultimately transient, global dominion fomented Mahan's theory of aggressive naval presence in support of a planet-wide network of merchant shipping assets and colonies as a means for promulgating geo-strategic supremacy for an aspirant nation.[27] For the British Empire of old, the Ship of the Line had provided the necessary muscle for their seventeenth through nineteenth century naval strategies. This paradigm was also emulated by other oceanic contenders, including France, Spain, and the United States. The tactical supremacy of these capital vessels remained unchallenged until the advent of steam-powered ironclad vessels such as the CSS Virginia, which dramatically debuted during the American Civil War at Hampton Roads.

Fortuitously, and through the prescience of her designer and champions, *Virginia's* archrival, the turreted USS *Monitor*, arrived in time to save her wooden siblings

[27] Ibid.

from a more prolonged demonstration of how tactical

supremacy could be wrought from shrewd embracement of

emergent technologies. What ensued thereafter amounted to a

technological arms race to produce the next capital ship,

which, for nations infused with the Mahan plan for world

domination (or at least regional hegemony), led down the

well-worn path of 'bigger is better' thinking. In the early

twentieth century, this meant heavily armored all-big-gun

dreadnaught battleships and battlecruisers, whose extreme

expense limited the number of nations that could afford and

maintain them to an industrialized few. It also limited the

number of such capital ships that each such nation could

sustain. Thus, the expense of essential naval assets necessary

to Mahan's theory, then as today, ensured that only wealthy

industrialized powers could pursue its implementation and

that they did so at the expense of diminished expenditure on

other naval assets and to great detriment to their national

budgets. To ensure that they were built and available for

deployment, the admiralties, legislators, and treasuries had to *believe* that Dreadnaughts were essential to their martial endeavors and surely invulnerable due to their design...and cost. Jobs, votes, funding, tradition, and pride demanded it, much as they continue to do for warships today.

The experience of the Russians at Tsushima in 1905 and of the British and Germans at Jutland in 1916 revealed, however, that not only were such large, armored vessels vulnerable to descending rounds and torpedoes, the loss of such ships in battle were indeed monetarily and collaterally expensive as well as harmful to national and fleet morale.[28] In fact, even though arguably tactically victorious at Jutland, the German High Seas Fleet never conducted a sortie *en mass* again in response to the losses they incurred during that melee.[29] The British public's morale reaction to the catastrophic loss of the revered HMS *Hood* to *Bismarck* in 1941 and the subsequent German fear of deploying *Tirpitz*

---

[28] John Campbell. Jutland: An Analysis of the Fighting. (London: Lyon Press, 1998), 231-233.

[29] Ibid, 234.

after the loss of *Bismarck* illustrated the psychological significance of such salient assets to a warring nation, with the loss or even potential loss of any one of these valuable assets negatively affected their sister-ship deployment options and consequently their efficacy and strategic value.[30] Too, In the case of the *Bismarck* and her sister ships, their expense and associated restrictions in numbers rendered their deployment options less flexible than a larger force of smaller ships might have provided –the latter potentially employing a greater capacity for concentration of force in space *or* time when nèeded over a less numerous capital ship-biased fleet, while enjoying increased survivability as a force *in toto*.

In fact, in both World Wars, Germany may have benefited significantly by greater investment in submarines than capital ships with such refocusing potentially dramatically altering the outcome of either war; in the first by

[30] Bruce Taylor. The Battlecruiser HMS Hood: An Illustrated Biography, 1916–1941. *(Annapolis, Maryland: Naval Institute Press, 2008), 224-226; John Sweetman. Tirpitz: Hunting the Beast (Gloucestershire, England: Sutton Publishing Limited, 2004, 16-17).*

breaking the Blockade and in the second by winning the Battle of the Atlantic. Not only was this reality portentous, but the latent ramification of a nation also fielding such an enhanced flexibility fleet was recognized by naval theorists and international negotiators during the interwar years.

In fact, the major sea powers negotiated limitations such as the Washington Naval Treaty of 1922, which tended to favor the more affluent parties that could afford the dreadnaughts over less affluent nations by limiting the number of lesser ships that could be built. This essentially created a "dreadnaught club" of seafaring hegemonic powers, most notably at this time the United States, England, France, Japan, Germany, and Italy. The limits in armament and tonnage of various classes of ships, ostensibly intended to forestall arms-races between these parties, therefore, served to perpetuate the supremacy of these wealthier and more resource affluent nations over any other potential contenders around the world.[31]

---

[31] "The Washington Naval Conference, 1921–1922."

Further, after limiting battleships to numbers they themselves could field, Britain and Japan sought to limit the number of *heavy cruisers* that the United States could build to ensure that they could remain competitive with the rising giant. Presciently, the British and Japanese apprehension at the time was that a much larger, flexible and survivable force of lesser capital ships that only the resource-rich Americans could deploy would facilitate the United States' Mahanesque aspirations to a greater extent than the fewer battleships and cruisers they themselves could afford.[32] Though it is seldom discussed, during this period of transition in naval supremacy from England to the United States, Britain's Prime Minister Lloyd George considered the possibility to preemptive war against the U. S. given that the new power was about to eclipse them and fulfill their Mahan-inspired dream of global hegemony.[33] The historical perspective here is that military

---

https://history.state.gov/nautical milestones/1921-1936/naval-conference (accessed January 3, 2015).

[32] Millett, et al, 351.

[33] Lynn Pcknett, Stephan Prior, and Clive Prince. Friendly Fire: The

theorists at the time understood the significance of such a force in pursuance of the Mahan hegemony paradigm.

However, as to the fate of the battleship itself, during this same period advancements in a new form of naval warfare were quietly taking place that rendered all these developments moot.

Secret War Between the Allies. (Edinburgh: Mainstream, 2005), 43-44.

The Rise of Naval Aviation

Though a U. S. Army aviator, Brigadier General William Mitchell was a fundamental contributor to the emergence of naval aviation, graphically - and famously - illustrating the vulnerability of the battleship to attack from the air in 1921.[34] For many of his contemporaries, the idea that the tiny, fragile, and relatively inexpensive airplane could pose a threat to monstrous, heavily armored, and expensive battleships seemed absurd. In fact, Captain William Leahy, speaking for the Navy following their own (rigged) tests,

---

[34] John T. Correll, "Billy Mitchell and the Battleships", Air Force Magazine, June 2008, 64–67.

stated that "the entire experiment pointed to the improbability of a modern battleship being either destroyed or completely put out of action by aerial bombs."[35] Even in the wake of Mitchell's successful demonstration, American naval planners rationalized and marginalized this new, and for them unpleasant, reality. British and Japanese observers, however, left Mitchell's demonstration quite impressed. Soon, the seeds of the construct took root their more fertile minds.

The British Royal Navy commissioned the first purpose-built aircraft carrier, HMS *Hermes*, in 1924, at the height of its naval-inspired contention with the United States. More significantly for the United States Navy the Japanese admiralty was provided by Mitchell with a means of projecting naval power beyond the constraints of the naval treaties that had also thus far frustrated their own Mahan-inspired aspirations.[36] Aircraft carriers were not covered by

[35] Ibid.

[36] Phillip Melinger, (Ed.). The Paths of Heaven: The Evolution of Air Power Theory. (Maxwell AFB, Alabama, Air University Press, 1997), 79–114.

standing agreements. Soon enough, the British action against the Italian fleet at Taranto and the Japanese against HMS *Prince of Wales* and *Repulse* and again against the U. S. fleet at Pearl Harbor revealed the battleship to be well-outmoded by 1941, with these events signaling the ascendancy of the carrier as the new principal capital ship and therefore the new primary instrument of Mahanesque geopolitical policy.

Wise to the evolutionary nature of warfare, the Imperial Japanese Navy adapted quickly, adopting the aircraft carrier as the new capital ship of their blue water fleet, entering the conflict with ten carriers to the Americans' seven. These they would employ to great effect in the opening phase of the war, but their advantage would dissipate rapidly as the U. S. Navy embraced the new carrier-centric paradigm, albeit begrudgingly and under duress, and with the incredible resource potential of the United States pressed into production several of the new capital ships.

For the United States Navy, both necessity and shocking reality forced a dependence on aircraft carriers to conduct the war against Japan. The American admiralty's error of marginalizing naval aviation and aircraft carriers in favor of the expensive and now suddenly eclipsed battleship was painfully manifested in the sixty-eight-minute assault on Pearl Harbor. However, the lesson was not lost on them: Fittingly, the first offensive naval action against Japan, Lieutenant Colonel James Doolittle's April 18, 1942 raid against Tokyo, not only originated from a carrier, USS *Hornet* (Roosevelt's "Shangri-La"), but was undertaken with B-25 "Mitchell" bombers, named after the maverick Army Air Service pioneer and battleship nemesis of the same name.[37]

Though this strategic carrier based strike was a "one-up," the reality "over the horizon" tactical carrier warfare was established at the Coral Sea engagement of May 8, 1942 and

embedded June 4-7, 1942 at Midway. Thus began the

[37] "The Halsey-Doolittle Raid" http://www.history.navy.mil/research/library/online-reading-room/title-list-alphabetically/h/halsey-doolittle-raid.html (accessed January 2, 2015).

dominance of the American carrier-centric air superiority and power projection naval strategy over all other surface force concepts for the duration of the conflict and beyond.[38]

In fact, with the bulk of the Japanese carrier force decimated by 1944, American carriers essentially took on the role of fleet air cover and strike missions for the duration of the war. It was in these final months of WWII that the carrier concept faced its greatest and contextually most historically relevant threats: The dive bomb, the torpedo, and the "kamikaze." Meaning "Divine Wind", the latter term referred to the fortuitous weather phenomenon that destroyed the massive invasion fleets of Kublai Khan in 1274 and 1281.[39]

[38] "The Battle of the Coral Sea" http://www.history.navy.mil/content/dam/nhhc/browse-by-topic/War%20and%20Conflict/The%20Battle%20of%20the%20Coral%20Sea/ww2-17.pdf (accessed January 2, 2015); "The Battle of Midway." http://www.history.navy.mil/research/library/online-reading-room/title-list-alphabetically/m/midways-strategic-lessons.html (accessed January 2, 2015).

[39] "The Kamikazes: Japanese Suicide Units." http://www.history.navy.mil/content/dam/nhhc/browse-by-topic/commemorations/commemorations-toolkits/wwii/articles-on-world-war-ii-naval-aviation/pdf/ww2-31.pdf (accessed January 2, 2016).

It was adapted to describe suicide pilots that attacked United States Navy forces in the last months of the war. The practitioners of the tactic were universally descendants of the warrior Samurai class and adherents to the self-sacrificing Bushido Code which advocated death before dishonor. It is this mindset of self-sacrifice that made them effective guidance systems for the first anti-ship guided missiles employed in war.

Most military plans involve three basic phases: Ingress, objective execution, and egress. Ingress is rather forthright; unless one considers the effect the desire to ultimately egress might have on resolve in this regard. In the case of the kamikaze, the lack of need for egress and the possession of a proficient, resolved, human guidance system rendered it a proto-cruise missile worthy of contextual consideration, given the concept's technological development into the unmanned Anti-Ship Cruise Missile (ASCM) of today. Other salient threats of the late WWII period such as the submarine, the torpedo and dive-bomb also augured unto perils that await the modern carrier in the twenty-first century. Extrapolations of these concepts such as the supercavitating torpedo and the Anti-Ship Ballistic missile (ASBM) pose emergent threats to the Supercarrier construct just as their ancestors did to the WWII carrier. For historical reference, *given the reality that the only actual combat experience involving carrier defense occurred during WWII*, an overview and comparison of carrier defenses and threats circa 1945 as well as more contemporary missile and aircraft combat events is warranted. As the focus here is the carrier and task force, analysis will be centered on the point protection of this element with escort defense reviewed given their place in the task force security. Though the United States Navy fielded many light and escort carriers, the emphasis here too will be on the fleet carriers, primarily of the Essex class, due to their historically analogous deployment with the modern *Nimitz* and *Ford* class Supercarriers.

WWII Combat Experience

3 Aftermath of Kamikaze Attack (Public Domain).

In 1945, as today, aircraft carriers were the most heavily defended naval assets in the US fleet. Nonetheless, of the twenty-four USN fleet carriers to see combat in WWII, five were lost to action [a 20.833% loss rate] of various kinds: CV-2 *Lexington* (dive-bombers/torpedo bombers), CV-5 *Yorktown* (torpedo bomber/submarine), CV-7 *Wasp* (submarine), CV-8 *Hornet* (dive bombers/torpedo bombers) and CV-23 *Princeton* (dive bomber). A further eight [33.33%

more of the fleet carrier capacity] were heavily damaged long enough to be put temporarily out of action: CV-3 *Saratoga* (submarine torpedo), CV-6 *Enterprise* (dive bomber/kamikaze), CV-9 *Essex* (kamikaze), CV-11 *Intrepid* (kamikaze), CV-13 *Franklin* (horizontally employed dive bomber), CV-*Ticonderoga* (kamikaze), CV-16 *Lexington* (submarine torpedo/kamikaze) and CV-17 *Bunker Hill* (kamikaze) with eight more [another 33.33%] extensively damaged.[40]

From this it can be derived that the empirical *existential* threats to the WWII United States fleet carrier in descending order were: Dive bombers (three kill participations, two heavy damages), torpedo bombers (three kill participations, one heavy damage), and submarines (two kill participations, one heavy damage). However, kamikazes were a significant and much dreaded threat to the carrier concept. These human-guided missiles accounted for or

[40] "World War Two Damage Reports and Photos" http://www.paperlessarchives.com/wwii_naval_damage_reports.html (accessed January 3, 2015).

contributed to sixteen instances of significant to heavy damage to United States fleet carriers of WWII (thus significantly damaging a total of 66.66% of the fleet carrier force).[41]

Though no fleet carriers were lost to kamikaze attacks, thirty-four USN ships of various types including three escort carriers and thirteen destroyers were sunk during the war by this means with 288 others significantly damaged (including the sixteen fleet carriers plus three light carriers, seventeen escort carriers and fifteen battleships); overall, 29.65% of the estimated 1,086 kamikaze attacks (out of 2,314 sorties – some turning back for various reasons) penetrated fleet defenses to hit their target.[42] Some 930 (out of 1,809 sorties) of these kamikaze attacks occurred over the seventy-seven-day Battle of Okinawa, April 6 through June 22, 1945, sinking seventeen American ships (including one escort carrier and ten destroyers) and damaging 198 others (including eight fleet

---

[41] "The Kamikazes: Japanese Suicide Units."

[42] Ibid.

carriers, four escort carriers and ten battleships). This equated to a successful penetration rate of 23.11%. In addition, six vessels were successfully attacked by the mission specific rocket propelled Ohka suicide aircraft which was essentially an air-launched human guided anti-ship cruise missile.[43]

Aircraft utilized for kamikaze attacks varied with availability. The Mitsubishi A6M "Zeke" with a terminal speed of over 350 kts and toting a 550-pound armor-piercing bomb (released just before impact) and the 250 kts Mitsubishi G4M "Betty" bomber packed with 2,000 pounds of explosive are indicative of the general employment. The "Ohka" rocket-plane, which had to be brought within twenty-three nautical miles of its target by modified "Betty" carrier planes, represented a high-end craft with a terminal velocity of 580 kts and a 1,700 lb. warhead. Conventional dive bombers generally delivered their 500-2,000 lb. bombs at over 300 kts and at high angles while torpedo bombers generally approached at 250 kts or less at low level and dropped their

[43] Ibid.

2,000 lb. (500 lb. warhead) torpedoes from 2,000 yards or less with a running speed of around forty-five knots. Submarines could fire their heavier (4,000 lb., with up to 1,000 lb. being warhead) torpedoes from as far as 6,000 yards with running speeds of up to fifty knots [suicide midget submarines having a similar performance].[44]

The efficacy of dive bomber munitions lay in their gravity-assisted vertical trajectory, allowing them to penetrate the relatively lightly armored flight decks of the American carriers. British carriers, with heavily armored flight decks, were less susceptible to this attack profile. Torpedoes, through the sheer volatility of their payloads, could and did break the keel and rupture the hulls of carriers. The kamikaze, however, with its lower-speed impact and lesser mass density, seldom penetrated the carriers' interiors and therefore could only create superficial, if extensive and temporarily incapacitating, damage on the massive ships.

---

[44] "The Kamikazes: Japanese Suicide Units."

Destroyers and other lesser vessels, however, could be, and were, sunk by single kamikazes on several occasions.

Against this onslaught, U. S. Navy vessels in WWII employed a variety of sensors, weapons, and tactics to provide for task force and individual point defense. Carrier defenses of 1945 began with the air wing itself, which provided long range patrol and reconnaissance, strike, and Air Cap that loitered near the Task Force. The Grumman F6F Hellcat, the premium and dominant US Navy fighter of the latter half of the war with a kill ratio of 19:1, had a maximum combat radius of 500 nautical miles with drop tanks and a ninety minute patrol time on station – calculated from a ferry range of 1,500 nautical miles, a cruise speed of 300 kts (388 kts being its maximum speed), a thrice-orbital patrol area fifty nautical miles in diameter and an internal fuel range of 950 nautical miles.[45] However, these aircraft were primarily employed much closer to the fleet, directed by radar and radio

---

[45] Leonard Bridgman, ed. "The Grumman Hellcat." Jane's Fighting Aircraft of World War II (London: Studio, 1946), 233-234.

from destroyers deployed in a fifty mile ring around the carrier force itself.

This aerial defense, known as the "Big Blue Blanket," was a tactical application developed by the inventor of the famous "Thatch Weave" air combat maneuver for fighter pilots, Lt. Commander John Thatch.[46] Air Cap linger time was dramatically increased to as much as four hours on patrol, with these patrols often stretching over the horizon from the destroyers (another fifty to sixty nautical miles depending on weather conditions). *Essex* class carriers nominally carried thirty-six air superiority Hellcats each. Radar equipped night-fighter versions were deployed after 1944, notably on the USS *Enterprise*; however, ship-based-radar-assisted day fighters were the primary tactical application throughout the closing stages of the conflict, and a vast preponderance of kamikaze attacks occurred in daylight. The detection range of the US

---

[46] Bill Coombes. "Divine Wind." The Commemorative Air Force Dispatch Online Archives, Spring 1995. http://rwebs.net/dispatch/output.asp?ArticleID=49 (accessed January 2, 2015).

Navy S-band search radar was limited to around twenty-five nautical miles for individual aircraft depending on weather conditions.[47] Radar provided the Navy with eyes in nocturnal or limited visibility environments and when linked to gun-training fire control systems provided increased accuracy in targeting both aircraft and surface vessels.

With intruder craft approaching at 300 kts (in the case of the A6M "Zeke"), threats were often detected seventy-five nautical miles from the carrier and up to twenty-five or so nautical miles from this outer destroyer ring, giving fifteen minutes response time before possible carrier/kamikaze interface. Orbiting Hellcats could be vectored to the inbound targets from their positions near the destroyers in as little as three to twelve minutes. Though enjoying a 19:1 kill ratio advantage over the combat-seeking "Zeke" by this time of the war – the kamikazes themselves would eschew aerial combat, delegating it to their escort fighters, and focus on their

---

[47] Norman Freidman. Naval Radars. (Annapolis, MD: Naval Institute Press, 1981), 84-114.

primary mission. Even when escorted, however, a substantial kamikaze attack could be thwarted at this stage by a well-directed, competent, and fortunate Air Cap.

As an example, on March 21, 1945, during the Battle of Okinawa, a kamikaze strike force of eighteen Betty bombers carrying "Ohka" suicide rocket-planes and twelve "Zeke" escort fighters approached Task Group 58.1. Thirty-six Hellcats were vectored by radio to intercept them seventy nautical miles from the carriers (some fifteen nautical miles from the outer-ring destroyers) downing them all during a twenty-minute battle and prior to the release option for the "Ohka's".[48] This, however, was not always the case given the unpredictable variables of air combat, disparate skill, visibility factors, position advantage, happenstance, and fortuity. Usual encounters at this juncture might involve four to twelve defending Hellcats against a larger force of "Zeke"-escorted kamikazes, perhaps eighteen to thirty-six, with twelve to twenty-four escorts indicative of the norm. Formations as

[48] "The Kamikazes: Japanese Suicide Units."

large as fifty-five kamikazes plus escort fighters were fielded at a time, though more commonly concentrations of force in time by smaller groups against dispersed targets were deployed.[49]

Attacking *en masse*, against reduced defenders and exploiting conditions as much as possible, 50% or more of attackers in the above force proportion example could penetrate this portion of the defenses, particularly considering the reality that each Hellcat could only carry 400 rounds of .50 caliber for each of its six guns (fired in unison), providing only thirty seconds of fire at 800 rpm. Thus, a theoretical attacking force of twelve kamikazes and six escorts, with the latter engaging at least six but likely more Hellcats and the former maneuvering to avoid targeting, might see the successful penetration of this outer ring of protective fighters by seven or eight kamikazes, a number supported by empirical evidence.[50]

[49] Ibid.

[50] Ibid.

These surviving aircraft next encountered the destroyers themselves (these often being targets for first-wave kamikazes to provide access to the carriers for follow on pilots, hence the high rate of destroyer losses to kamikazes). *Fletcher* class destroyers, the dominant class of U. S. Navy destroyers in WWII (175 being built), possessed five single 5"/38 guns, up to ten 40 mm guns and as many as ten 20 mm guns.[51] This enhanced anti-aircraft capability over pre-war configurations was a direct development of the increased threat capacity of naval aviation as demonstrated by incidents such as the December 10, 1941 Japanese sinking of the HMS *Prince of Wales* and *Repulse* and through early American experience in the South Pacific.[52]

The 5"/38 caliber gun with the Mark 37 Gun Fire Control System could effectively engage aircraft out to 10,000

---

[51] Norman Friedman. *US Destroyers: An Illustrated Design History (Revised Edition). (Annapolis MD: Naval Institute Press, 2004), 111-118, 472.*

[52] Martin Middlebrook and Patrick Mahoney. Battleship: The Sinking of the Prince of Wales and the Repulse. (New York: Charles Scribner's Sons, 1979), 172-177.

yards at fifteen degree elevation (roughly the short range of the S-band radar) at fifteen to twenty-two rounds per minute per barrel, with an empirical average of 100 rounds required to destroy each enemy aircraft using the VT proximity fuse round.[53] The Bofors 40 mm L/60, meanwhile, had a range of 7,500 yards and a service ceiling of 23,500 feet with a rate of fire of 120 rounds per minute per barrel (though an effective range of 4,000 yards and an 80-100 rpm rate of fire was found to be nominal due to the need to manually load the shell strips and aiming considerations).[54] Possessing a mechanical gun control system and radar coordination via com-link, the 40 mm's aiming nonetheless relied on the venerable "Mark 1 Eyeball" with its well-established limitations. Incoming kamikazes that survived the torrent above would generally be specifically targeting the destroyers themselves and would

---

[53] Tony Diguilian. *"United States of America: 5"/38 (12.7 cm) Mark 12" http://www.navweaps.com/Weapons/WNUS_5-38_mk12.htm (accessed January 3, 2015).*

[54] David Zats. "Bofors Guns of World War II." 2001. http://www.allpar.com/history/military/bofors.html (accessed January 3, 2015).

therefore next encounter the 20 mm Oerlikon cannon with a maximum effective range against aircraft of about 1,000 yards and a practical rate of fire of around 300 rpm.[55]

The above data gives us an average firing rate of ninety 5" rounds per minute between 10,000 and 7,500 yards out, which with a target closure rate of 300 kts (150 yards per second) allows for a sixteen second window of fire prior to 40 mm engagement, with only twenty-five rounds capable of being fired, and therefore only a 25% possibility of kill on average employing VT proximity fuse ammunition against a single target (this assuming a broadside by all five guns; from end on with only two guns available, this drops to ten rounds and a ten percent kill probability - albeit the cross sectional area of the ship is reduced thus diminishing kamikaze impact probability). More than one kamikaze approaching at the

---

[55] "United States of America 20 mm/70 (0.79") Marks 2, 3 & 4." December 2015. http://www.navweaps.com/Weapons/WNUS_2cm-70_mk234.htm (accessed January 3, 2015).

same time and from a different vector would halve this figure again, while four reduces this by a factor of two yet again.

Given that the destroyers had to be spaced no more than twelve nautical miles apart in a circle of fifty nautical miles (a 160 nautical mile perimeter) to provide an unbroken circle of anti-aircraft protection, thirteen to fourteen destroyers would be required for this mission alone, with a roughly three-mile space between ships where only 5" guns could provide cover even in the best-case scenario (often fewer destroyers than this were available). These "gaps," of course, would be visible to the carrier-bound kamikazes who would attempt to exploit them to avoid the denser 40 mm fire closer to the destroyers, thus providing a successful penetration rate of 75-90% of post-first line-fighter carrier defenses depending on the gunnery angle of the defending ships. This explains the high loss rate of destroyers, a total of nineteen, to kamikaze attacks.

The successful penetration rate declined dramatically where two or more destroyers could provide overlapping 5" gunfire, with two ships diminishing it to 50-80% and three to 25-70%. Assuming averages, a carrier bound destroyer-evading kamikaze that had survived interception by the outer-ring fighters had a 65% chance of penetrating toward the inner Task Force defenses. This factor reduces the initial attacking force of twelve kamikazes to four or five.

U. S. Navy CV task forces were numerically large compared to modern carrier task forces. Task Group 58.1 on March 21, 1945 (from the incident noted above), numbered two fleet carriers, two light carriers, two battleships, six cruisers, and eighteen destroyers.[56] Subtracting the fourteen destroyers necessary for perimeter patrol, the inner force would have four destroyers available. These four destroyers would be deployed in a fifteen nautical mile diameter circle to provide the same interlinking coverage as the outer ring, thus

[56] "US Carrier Task Force 58." 1992. http://carl.army.mil/nafziger/944UFNA.pdf (accessed January 11, 2016).

positioned some five nautical miles from the carriers. Given

the ability to maneuver in response to the approaching aircraft

and provide overlapping five-inch and interlacing 40 mm and

20 mm fire, these destroyers would provide an additional

diminishing factor giving a thus-far successful single

kamikaze a less than 50% chance of advancing beyond *this*

point, thereby reducing the terminal carrier-bound attack force

to a probable two or three. These two or three surviving

kamikazes from an initial force of twelve provides a realistic

theoretical manifestation of the empirical 23.11% successful

penetration rate against prepared combat forces during the

Battle of Okinawa.[57]

These last two or three aircraft faced the point

defenses of the carriers themselves. These consisted, in thecae

of the dominant *Essex* class, of twelve 5" guns in four twin

mounts and four single mounts; up to eighteen Mk-12 Quad

40 mm (72 guns total) mounts and up to seventy-six single 20

---

[57] Lawrence *Sowinski, "The Essex Class Carriers" Warships*
Volume II. (Annapolis, MD: Naval Institute Press, 2000), 30, 97.

mm cannon.[58] This arsenal vomited a veritable wall of over 30,250 rounds per minute (of all calibers) emanating from ninety-eight guns (264 5", 7,200 40 mm and 22,800 20 mm per minute). In broadside, these numbers were halved save for the four twin 5" turrets which, being mounted fore and aft of the island, could be trained in either direction (roughly 15,500 rpm total). The end-on numbers were reduced to two twin 5", two single 5", four quad 40 mm and around twenty 20 mm (roughly 7,750 rpm).

With a terminal approach velocity of 150 yards per second, kamikazes provided the 5" anti-aircraft defense gunners with less than sixty seconds to fire from the time the target came within range until impact. The 40 mm gunners had about forty seconds to engage and the 20 mm gunners about six seconds. This meant that when a single kamikaze approached the broadside of an *Essex* class fleet carrier it could expect 200 five-inch, 2,400 40 mm and 11,400 20 mm rounds to come its way during the last minute of its existence.

---

[58] Ibid.

Amazingly, and significantly to our later discussion, kamikazes were able to penetrate this last line of defenses as well (sometimes with deceased pilots and sheer momentum), causing extensive damage to sixteen of twenty-four fleet carriers.

As an historical example, on May 11, 1945, as part of the immense *Kikusui Rokugi Sakusen* ("Floating Chrysanthemums") kamikaze operation during the Battle of Okinawa, two surviving "Zeke" kamikazes from a flight of six (33.33%) penetrated task force defenses and severely damaged CV-17 *Bunker Hill*, killing 346 men, with forty-three missing and 264 wounded.[59] Albeit this attack occurred while resting at Condition One, the incident did occur within the combat zone. The casualties mostly resulted from fire caused by the ruptured tanks of aircraft parked on the flight deck as well as their own ammunition, a primary threat to

---

[59] "Bunker Hill, CV-17."
http://www.history.navy.mil/research/histories/ship-histories/danfs/b/bunker-hill-i.html (accessed January 11, 2016).

aircraft carriers as illustrated by the Japanese experience at the Battle of Midway.[60]

As illustrated here and in other notable examples (USS *Franklin*, *Yorktown*, et al) a stricken aircraft carrier was prone to fires and sympathetic explosions, given the extensive stocks of aviation fuel and munitions that were required by the air wing. Penetration of the flight deck by armor-piercing gravity bombs often led to internal chain reaction explosions from these stocks. (This threat would remain evident in the late 1960s with the USS *Oriskany*, *Forrestal* and *Enterprise* incidents that are discussed in some detail below). A secondary threat was flooding from a ruptured hull, usually the result of torpedo damage, which caused heavy listing and required complicated damage control operations.

Incapacitation of a carrier portended to loss of air combat capacity and the resultant vulnerability of the rest of

[60] "The Battle of Midway."
http://www.history.navy.mil/research/library/online-reading-room/title-list-alphabetically/m/midways-strategic-lessons.html (accessed January 2, 2015).

the task force which is why WWII fleet carriers usually operated in groups of two to four. Efficient fire and damage control were crucial to the survival of stricken ships. Yet the survivability of a ship often lays in its design. Armor ranging from two and a half inches on the flight deck to four inches at the hull waterline as well as critical systems redundancy, compartmentalization and damage control procedures reduced the effects of successful attacks on *Essex* class carriers but could not save stricken ships in all cases. As mentioned, British carriers, with thicker deck armor, were less susceptible than the American carriers to vertical penetration and therefore enjoyed a greater degree of survivability to dive bombing and kamikaze attacks, yet, with relatively thin hull armor, were equally susceptible to torpedoes.[61]

Torpedoes contributed to the sinking of four of five lost fleet carriers (CV-2 *Lexington*, CV-5 *Yorktown,* CV-7 *Wasp*, and CV-8 *Hornet*) and the heavy damaging of two (CV-3 *Saratoga* and CV-16 *Lexington*), both being attacked

[61] "The Kamikazes: Japanese Suicide Units."

by submarine. Three aircraft-borne torpedoes and three dive bombs led to the sinking of *Hornet*, while three dive bombs and two submarine torpedoes sank *Yorktown*. Two dive-bombs and two airborne torpedoes sank the first *Lexington* (CV-2), and three submarine torpedoes sank CV-7 *Wasp*. Japanese submarines successfully evaded destroyer escorts and attacked four of the fleet carriers, sinking *Wasp*, contributing to the sinking of *Yorktown* and heavily damaging *Saratoga* and CV-16 *Lexington*.[62]

As an additional historical context, kamikaze watercraft in the guise of the 400 *Shinyo* class high-speed (30 plus kts) motor boats with 500 pound warheads and several midget submarines laden with up to 2,000 pounds of explosives were employed against the American fleet at Okinawa, the former sinking or heavily damaging twenty-one support ships and the latter five (a success rate of less than 5% but worthy of contemporary consideration given the USS

[62] "World War Two Damage Reports and Photos" http://www.paperlessarchives.com/wwii_naval_damage_reports.html (accessed January 3, 2015).

Cole incident and the potential for conflict in the Straits of
Hormuz and other constricted waterways).[63] A swarm of such

vessels bearing anti-ship missiles could potentially
overwhelm the defenses of any vessel in constricted water.

The experience of the Imperial Japanese Navy is also
worth consideration. The Japanese entered the war with ten
aircraft carriers of various sizes, including six fleet carriers,
compared to the United States' total of seven diverse carriers.
Embracing naval aviation from its nativity, the Japanese
strategy for the opening phases of the war was carrier-centric,
including the nearly decisive strike against the American fleet
at Pearl Harbor. Though initially successful, the loss of four
fleet carriers during the Battle of Midway seriously
diminished the Japanese capacity after 1942, and valuable
vessels, aircraft and trained personnel became irreplaceable
for them. In total, the Japanese lost twenty-one aircraft

---

[63] "The Kamikazes: Japanese Suicide Units."

carriers out of a total force of twenty-five, with thirteen fleet carriers sunk out of the fourteen employed during the war.[64]

The experience of the last generation of battleships during the Second World War must also be considered. Thick armor, compartmentalization and sheer mass often failed to protect them from sinking caused by torpedo or dive-bomb or even the very battleship shells that they were designed to counter. The instantaneous loss of the Battlecruiser HMS *Hood* to descending projectiles, the incapacitation of the German *Bismarck* by an aerial torpedo and the fate of the colossal *Yamato* speak to the vulnerability of even the most powerful and heavily armored vessels.

One cannot help but conclude from this historical analysis that aircraft carriers, the largest and most heavily defended warships of the war, proved just as vulnerable to attack as their heavily armored battleship cousins were, with

---

[64] *David Evans and Mark Peattie. Kaigun: Strategy, tactics, and technology in the Imperial Japanese Navy, 1887–1941. (Annapolis, MD: Naval Institute Press, 1997), 315-323.*

their defenses ultimately subject to penetration regardless of the mass and efficacy of their firepower (and that of their escorts) and that neither armor nor compartmentalization or even sheer mass preventing them from sinking or being put out of action when struck. Not only were seemingly impenetrable task force and point defenses penetrated on multiple occasions, but warhead impacts also caused substantial damage to these massive, armored and heavily compartmentalized warships. History's lessons regarding these occurrences could not be clearer:

1) *All weapons and military constructs including capital ship types and the tactics and strategies they inspire become obsolete in time.*

2) *No vessel or type of vessel is invulnerable in combat and the psychological impact of losing even one of a limited number of such capital ships not only damages national and force morale but constrains the future deployment of like assets for fear of endangering more; factors which serve to limit the employment options and therefore efficacy of the force in toto.*

3) *Militaries that adapt quickest and fullest to emergent technologies and dynamic geostrategic realities have a distinct advantage in warfare.*

A further lesson might be the erroneous precept of investing so heavily in battleships at all given the theoretical supremacy of a more numerous and therefore more flexible and survivable force of smaller vessels in concentration of force in time and/or space applications as well as in pursuance of a Mahanesque naval-centric geostrategic foreign policy. It was this reality, ironically, that led to the Naval Treaties of the 1920s. These indices must be considered in contemplating future force procurement expenditures in the modern age.

Post War Developments

4 Jets shorten response time...in both directions (Public Domain).

The United States Navy emerged from WWII with ninety-nine aircraft carriers including twenty-eight fleet carriers and seventy-one escort carriers. These vessels formed the core of 6.768 ship fleet that included twenty-three battleships, seventy-two light and heavy cruisers, 377 destroyers, 361 frigates, 232 submarines, 586 mine warfare vessels, 1,204 coastal patrol boats, 2,547 amphibious assault ships, and 1,267 auxiliary and support vessels.[65] By 1946 this

[65] "Ship Force Levels." 1946. http://www.history.navy.mil/research/histories/ship-histories/us-ship-force-levels.html (accessed February 14, 2016).

massive force had been downsized to 1,248 ships total including only fifteen fleet carriers and ten escort carriers supported by ten battleships, 36 cruisers, 145 destroyers, thirty-five frigates, eighty-five submarines, 112 mine warfare vessels, 119 coastal patrol boats, 275 amphibious assault ships and 406 auxiliary support vessels.[66] By June 1947 this force had been again reduced to a total of 842 ships, built around fourteen fleet carriers and eight escort carriers. Battleships were reduced to only four, reflecting the acceptance of their obsolescence in the new age. This downsizing in the immediate wake of WWII resulted from the (as it turned out, unwarranted) overt confidence in the capacity of nuclear weaponry to deter aggression, as well as the national weariness of war.

The mindset of Americans can be forgiven during this period, given their unilateral possession of atomic weapons in the immediate wake of World War Two. Yet the reality was that until 1949, the United States possessed very few of the

[66] Ibid.

new weapons and those that existed could not be stored in ready form and had to be assembled just prior to deployment to prevent over-heating of the components. For instance, in 1948, the U. S. possessed only fifty Mark 3 "Fat Man" type weapons and only thirty-three USAF aircraft modified to carry them.[67] This because the weapons tended to start heating up when assembled and therefore could not be kept on "stand by".[68] Further, each weapon required two days assembly by a thirty-nine-man crew of which there was only one.

Since overheating began immediately upon assembly of the components, delivery of the weapon to target – or disarming by the same exclusive team – had to occur within hours of completion. Ergo, only one weapon could be made deliverable at a time at first. Even by 1951, though with 550 Mark 4's on hand (which *could* be pre-assembled and stored),

[67] William Arkin and Peter Pringle. SIOP: The Secret US Plan for Nuclear War. (New York: W.W. Norton, 1983), 56-62.

[68] Ronald Powaski. The March Toward Armageddon. (Oxford: Oxford University Press, 1987), 53-59.

there were only 114 aircraft altered and detailed to carry the 10,850 lb. weapon.[69]

From the perspective of potential adversaries, the likelihood of the United States deploying atomic weaponry again so soon after their introduction at Hiroshima and Nagasaki - particularly in an asymmetric conflict against a much lesser nation - was practically zero. This perception, combined with a massive reduction of American conventional military assets and personnel created an environment of 'paper deterrence' that encouraged the North Korean invasion of South Korea in 1950. The Korea Conflict saw the employment of the carrier primarily in interdiction, close air support (notably at Chosin Reservoir), air strikes in the North and in maintaining air superiority over the peninsula. Direct threats to these vessels during this time frame were non-extent, providing us, therefore, with only offensive action data for this period. At the initiation of hostilities, the U. S. Navy

---

[69] Walter Poole. The History of the Joint Chiefs of Staff, Vol. IV (1950-1952). (New York: Amazon, 2012), 534.

possessed only eleven fleet carriers (three being the new 45,000-ton *Midway* class – though none of these three were deployed to Korea during this period – the other eight *Essex* class) and one battleship, USS *Missouri*, as part of a 634-ship fleet.[70] Jet aircraft such as the F2H Banshee and F9F Panther were employed to great effect from the *Essex* class carriers during the Korean War.

Meanwhile, the trend of carrier deployment manifest in the Korean War would continue through the Vietnam Era and beyond, that is without any direct threats challenging the carrier's presence in the theater (save for the potential of Soviet naval interference). However, incapacitating accidents involving three fleet carriers, the U.S.S. *Oriskany*, *Forrestal* and *Enterprise*, the circumstances of which will be discussed below, illustrate the continued vulnerability of these complex platforms to even relatively minor events.

---

[70] "Ship Force Levels."

In the early 1950s, American aircraft carrier designers incorporated the combat experiences of WWII fleet carriers into their design considerations, with survivability of the increasingly expensive and therefore increasingly fewer ships a priority. Advanced carriers based on WWII experience, such as the Midway class and the 53,000-ton *Forrestal* class, conventional in power but with angled flight decks, jet-blast deflectors, optical landing aids, catapults and other advancements that would form the Supercarrier were fielded in the years following the war. Most of the surviving *Essex* class vessels were modified during this period to include the adaptations, with these new technologies substantially increasing the capacity of the warships to conduct their primary missions. However, the existential threats to the aircraft carrier, the vertically delivered armor-piercing incendiary, the torpedo, and the kamikaze, all proven to be capable of incapacitating fleet-sized carriers, also emerged from WWII ripe for infusion with new technologies. So, too, did their primary deployment platforms, the aircraft, and the submarine.

While jet propulsion provided the carriers with increased punch and defense capacity, it also increased the approach rate and delivery capability of potential attackers, including the new cruise missiles that would soon fill the arsenals of the Soviet Union. Faster closure rates meant less response time. Advancements in radar, infrared and other terminal guidance systems increased the likelihood of an attacking missile making contact should it penetrate point defenses, while at the same time providing defenders with increased likelihood of mitigating the threat. Submarine technology, too, saw advancement in performance and duration, with the eventual development of nuclear propulsion providing the capacity to stalk vessels for practically unlimited periods of time. Championed by Admiral Hyman Rickover, nuclear power, for all intents and purposes, gave underwater vessels unlimited range and linger capacity. When applied to the aircraft carrier, in the guise of the

95,000-ton CVN-65 *Enterprise* class a whole new breed of vessel was created.

The Supercarrier

<u>5</u> CVN-65 Enterprise, the first Supercarrier (Public Domain).

The advent of nuclear propulsion provided the carrier with practically unlimited range (jet fuel, munitions and food being the only real constraints), while advancements in radar and other electronic technologies rendered the carrier an all-weather day and night platform for naval aviation operations. Designers were gifted with immense power for catapults, propulsion and electronics allowing for many improvements on the preceding designs. These improvements ultimate manifested themselves in the ten *Nimitz* class Supercarriers, first deployed in 1975, which are currently dominant in the United States Navy's inventory and only now (2018) being replaced by the even more impressive *Ford* class CVN.

At 1,094 feet in length and 252 feet in width, the 110,000 plus ton *Nimitz* class dwarfs the 862 foot long by 147 foot wide 30,800-ton *Essex* class.[71] With almost twice the crew (5,500 or more versus 3,200) to protect, the *Nimitz* class carriers feature state of the art point defenses, or Close in Weapons Systems (CIWS), in the form of radar and infrared guided anti-missile missiles and Phalanx Gatling guns.

Like their conventional post-war predecessors, the nuclear-powered *Nimitz* class Supercarriers have primarily served as strike platforms, aggressive diplomatic tools and humanitarian aid support vessels with their tactical presence remaining essentially unchallenged since World War Two.

This means that there is little empirical information regarding

[71] Lawrence *Sowinski, "The Essex Class Carriers" Warships Volume II (Annapolis, MD: Naval Institute Press, 2000), 97; Norman Polmar, The Naval Institute Guide to the Ships and Aircraft of the U.S. Fleet (Annapolis, Maryland: Naval Institute Press, 2004), 108-113.*

defensive actions on the part of Supercarriers. However, empirical data regarding successful anti-ship missile and torpedo attack as well as damage efficacy against lesser vessels does exist, as well as results from defensive weapons performance testing that have been made public.

Additionally, information regarding the capacity of electronic detection, targeting and countermeasures exists in varying degrees of declassification with some empirical data also extent from late twentieth and early twenty-first century conflicts. Further, data exists concerning the three current existential threats to the modern nuclear Supercarrier concept, namely the hypersonic anti-ship cruise missile, the ballistic anti-ship missile and the super-cavitating torpedo – all of which are being fielded by the primary potential naval adversaries of the United States Navy: China, Russia, and Iran. Lastly, empirical experience from accidents aboard the U.S.S. *Forrestal, Oriskany*, and *Enterprise* Supercarriers reveal the vulnerability and even fragility of these massive ships.

The 1966, USS *Oriskany* accident, caused by a magnesium flare, the 1967 USS *Forrestal* accident and the 1969 *Enterprise* accident (both of the latter resulting from single seventy-nine pound Zuni Rocket -with a fifteen pound warhead - misfires) indicate that incapacitation of such large vessels is likely in the case of fire and explosion.[72] They further indicate that only a small amount of incendiary or explosives (less than 15 lbs. in all three cases) are necessary to incapacitate the vessel and therefore its attached air arm. These incidents resulted in the loss of forty-four, 134 and twenty-eight dead respectively, with a loss of fifteen aircraft in the case of *Enterprise*. All three ships were put out of action for an extended period. This means that size alone is not a guarantee of combat survivability.

Lesser nations with potential of malignant interaction with American carrier forces include North Korea and Iran,

[72] "USS Forrestal (CVA-59). http://www.navy.mil/navydata/nav_legacy.asp?id=64 (accessed January 25, 2016); "Enterprise Remembers 1969 Fire." http://www.navy.mil/submit/display.asp?story_id=64783 (accessed January 25, 2016).

both of which field extensive fleets of small craft that may be employed in swarm attacks, notably by the Iranians in the Persian Gulf given its restricted terrain. Both, also, like the Chinese, field modern diesel-electric attack submarines, which are much quieter than their nuclear counterparts and therefore dangerous to U. S. Navy assets especially when armed with super-cavitating torpedoes or hypersonic cruise missiles. These vessels have revealed a capacity for penetrating carrier task force defenses even as late as 2008.

The area denial capacity of ballistic anti-ship missiles and hypersonic cruise missiles portent to limitations in Supercarrier deployment options in the future, forcing them too far from potential objectives, thereby mitigating their efficacy. Combined with high development, construction, maintenance and operational costs and the resultant limitations in numbers available (the USN only fields ten such vessels) - as well as the potential for a morale-damaging loss, questioning of the viability of continued investment in the

Supercarrier concept is as warranted today as were similar

discussions regarding battleships in the 1930s.

Emerging Threats

6 Mobile Ballistic Missile Launcher (Public Domain).

The Chinese mobile land-based DF-26 ballistic anti-ship missile, for instance, can reach 2,200 nautical miles from the east coast of China. This allows them to target U. S. bases in Japan and Guam. The DF-26 carries the WU-14 Hypersonic Glide Vehicle (HGV) armed with a tactical nuclear or armor-piercing conventional warhead and AI-assisted terminal guidance.[73]   Their range and their mobile domestically-based deployment provides the Chinese with

---

[73] "U.S. Navy Sees Chinese HGV as Part of Wider Threat." (http://aviationweek.com/awin/us-navy-sees-chinese-hgv-part-wider-threat (accessed January 23, 2016).

andante-Access/Area Denial (A2/AD) capacity in the waters extending 2,200 nautical miles from their coast – beyond the range of unrefueled carrier strike aircraft. Being mobile in urban or difficult rural terrain, pre-emptive or retaliatory action would be difficult if not impossible given the unlikelihood of locating them prior to launch signature (recall the American 1990 'Scud hunting' experience of the First Gulf War, conducted in open desert), their home-field defenses and the escalatory nature of attacking military assets on the Chinese mainland. [74] Hence, through the very existence of the DF-26/WU-14, the Chinese have achieved *de facto* A2/AD of a substantial portion of the Western Pacific.

Deployment of these assets on islands in the South China Sea, artificial or otherwise, would equally exclude areas extending 2,200 nautical miles in radius from these points (though they would become easier to preemptively target tactically or to retaliate against geo-politically). Too, the development of this technology into a sea-launched

[74] Ibid.

capacity (by altering extent SLBM's in Chinese ballistic missile submarines to carry a WU-14 derivative for instance, or adaptation of the DF-26/WU-14 to surface combatants or merchant vessels) could extend this capacity to a global threat.

The effects and consequences of a tactical nuclear strike are obvious, although one may cogitate that the use of sub-kiloton tactical nuclear weapons at sea (particularly underwater) may be less likely to escalate into global thermonuclear war than attacks against land targets. Therefore, the payload for any employed weapon in a naval conflict would likely be conventional, incendiary and armor-piercing. Striking vertically on the carrier flight deck with a terminal velocity of a mile a second (5,280 fps, 3,600 kts), the kinetic energy of a WU-14 size vehicle on impact is calculated by the Australian Strategic Policy Institute to generate the equivalent energy release of an American Harpoon anti-ship missile (488 lbs. HE warhead), though conventional WU-14 warhead would likely be of high-density armor-piercing depleted uranium incendiary design to assure penetration and maximum damage.[75]

Modern Supercarriers, at 100,000 tons and more, are highly compartmentalized, with multiple redundancies, superb damage control capabilities and highly trained crews. Given the historical efficacy of vertically impacting armor-piercing bombs on American fleet carriers, causing, or contributing to the sinking of three of five such vessels lost in WWII, it is likely that a single conventional WU-14 would render the vessel ineffective for an extended period. The effect of the two kamikazes that incapacitated U.S.S. *Bunker Hill* during WWII seems analogous.

There is little experience regarding the employment of the Harpoon against large vessels. In fact, the salient example of the use of the Harpoon missile against a ship of any size is the April 18, 1988 sinking of the British-built 1,540-ton Iranian frigate *Sahan* by United States Navy assets during

---

[75] "U.S. Navy Sees Chinese HGV as Part of Wider Threat."

Operation Praying Mantis. Though only 1.54% of the mass of

the *Nimitz* class Supercarrier, the *Sahan* required three

Harpoon missiles as well as two AGM-123 Skipper II

missiles (a laser guided, rocket assisted, 1,000 lb. Mk-83

General Purpose bomb) and two Rockeye cluster bombs.[76]

While the 4,850-ton HMS *Sheffield* only one Exocet anti-ship

cruise missile (1,450 lb. warhead) to sink it during the 1982

Falkland War, this vessel still only represents 4% of the mass

of a Supercarrier.[77] With this in consideration, some may be

inclined to argue that the very size of the carrier is its primary

asset. Recall here, however, that three American Pseudo

Supercarriers, *Forrestal, Oriskany*, and *Enterprise,* have been

incapacitated by as little as 15 lbs. of munitions.

---

[76] "Operation Praying Mantis: A Look Back at How U.S. Naval
Forces Responded to Hostile Forces in the Arabian Gulf."
http://www.navy.mil/ah_online/ftrStory.asp?id=73470 (accessed
January 25, 2015).

[77] Sandy Woodward and Patrick Robinson. *One Hundred Days:
The Memoirs of the Falklands Battle Group Commander. (London:
Naval Institute Press, 1997), 8.*

This means that the Supercarrier is vulnerable to ASBM attack, with destruction certain in the case of a single nuclear armed WU-14 (estimated 0.3 kiloton), or to incapacitating damage by a single lucky hit or multiple hits of a conventional variant. Future generations of the DF-26/WU-14 concept may pack a larger punch through employment of thermo baric (fuel-air) munitions without sacrificing size and terminal velocity.

In fact, the massive size of the ship, one may counter-argue, is its primary weakness as far as the ballistic anti-ship missile scenario is concerned, being difficult to conceal from a terminal guidance system (infra-red and active/semi-active and passive emissions radar, image matching or Light Detection and Ranging (LIDAR) approaching vertically.

Even at thirty-five knots, a vessel could only travel twenty-two nautical miles in the thirty-six-minute flight time at the maximum 2,200 nautical miles range of the DF-26/WU-14. Such a warhead, at 300,000 feet altitude, with a seeker head radius of 22.5 degrees, would have a terminal guidance sight circle of 40 nautical miles in diameter centered on the initial targeting point data and thus a 'threat ring' covering 400 square nautical miles of ocean surface. Given that such attacks are likely to be launched in salvos it is probable that at least some warheads that navigated the "kill chain" from target detection to impact approach would acquire the vessel.

This kill chain includes initial targeting of the vessel, midcourse correction at peak exoatmospheric altitude and terminal guidance, all potentially executed by networked surface, subsurface, airborne, and space-based military assets. Artificial Intelligence may allow future HGVs to evade defenses and not only learn from its experiences but share them with other missiles in the attacking swarm in real time.

To counter this, the Supercarrier task force has multiple defenses including not only aircraft, the Aegis Air Defense System and CIWS self-defense, but also surface, subsurface, drone and space-based assets at its disposal integrated into a networked defensive construct known as the

Cooperative Engagement Capability. This is an updated version of the Big Blue Blanket concept with airborne radar and integrated and networked multi-platform fire control systems among task force ships and aircraft multiplying the system's capacity for engagement.

Interruption of the kill chain is currently being addressed by the U. S. Navy to include Anti-Satellite and Anti-Ballistic Missile intercepts by Aegis-based Standard 3 missiles which have demonstrated an intercept rate of 84.2% for ASBM.[78] The Aegis system has the capacity to track and potentially engage over 100 targets at once at 100 nautical miles, limited only by the missile stock at hand and rate of fire available, as well as response-to-threat time. Other options that are being considered for carrier point ASBM defense are laser-based systems and shotgun inspired rail guns firing depleted uranium pellets that shred the incoming missiles at the last possible moment.[79]

[78] "Aegis Ballistic Missile Defense" http://www.mda.mil/system/aegis_bmd.html (accessed January 22, 2016).

The Chinese YJ-12 anti-ship cruise missile (ASCM)

carries a 1,100 lb. armor piercing warhead (the same weight

as Skipper II) or a low-yield nuclear device with terminal

velocities of Mach 3 (2,300 kts/3,400 fps) at ranges up to 250

nautical miles. Such weapons can be carried by multiple

platforms, including aircraft, surface vessels and submarines.

Chinese naval literature outlining anti-carrier tactics indicate

an interest in multi-axial saturation assaults by such means

(thus the likelihood of similar salvo attacks by ASBM).[80]

Lastly, the supercavitating torpedo, which allows for

incredible underwater speeds, also shortens reaction time for

defenders. Given the lethality demonstrated by torpedoes

during WWII against fleet carriers, a dearth of anti-torpedo

defensive technologies and the potential fanaticism of its

applicants – who may be willing to sacrifice a vessel and crew

---

[79] Ibid.

[80] "Document: China's Military Strategy."
http://news.usni.org/2015/05/26/document-chinas-military-strategy
(accessed January 25, 2015).

to sink or incapacitate an American Supercarrier – such devices must be taken into consideration.

What follows are viable contemporary scenarios influenced by the empirical combat experience of WWII, the strategic and tactical theories of the primary potential naval adversaries, China, Russia, Iran, and North Korea and those of the United States will be considered:

Modern Attack/Defense Scenario 1: ASBM

An American carrier task force operating within the 2,200-mile range of mobile DF-26 batteries in China would likely be engaged by them should conflict erupt. Counter-options are limited since preemptive or even retaliatory strikes against the Chinese mainland portend to nuclear escalation. Such is the basis of the Chinese A2/AD strategy, denying American power projection into their region. This strike would likely be a coordinated saturation attack given the large number of dispersed but networked launchers available. As many as 120 dispersed missiles launches could be initiated

given the significance of the target, which as noted, could

have only moved less than 25 miles during their flight time.

Approaching the carrier group from on high at a

reentry speed of Mach 10 (over 10,000 fps), the WU-14s

would only allow carrier defenses a minute to engage with the

SM-3 during the terminal phase. Assuming a launch rate of

two SM-3 launches per second per escort vessel, twenty-four

SM-3s per vessel and five vessels total, the Aegis based

Cooperative Engagement Capable task force would be able to

fire 120 SM-3s in that engagement period. With an

established kill rate of 84.2%, the group could only destroy

102 incoming missiles in this period. This leaves eighteen

warheads for the CIWS itself – Phalanx and Sea Sparrow, et

al, to engage with at least four to six WU-14's likely

penetrating to hit the carrier (a 4% penetration rate). To

survive such an assault, modern Supercarrier groups will need

higher volumes of ABM missiles and improved CIWS. Given

the historic peril of the dive bomb to the carrier designs of

WWII, the ASBM, essentially an extrapolation of this construct, is an existential threat to the Supercarriers.

Though emphasis is placed on disrupting the DF-26/WU-14 kill chain, possibly via exoatmospheric engagement of Chinese tracking satellites, should any payload vehicles successfully navigate these disruptions and achieve interface, incapacitation of the Supercarrier target is almost certain.

Modern Attack/Defense Scenario 2: Air Launched ASCM

Given the Chinese military's predilection for saturation attacks, one might also imagine a multi-axial attack by thirty-six YJ-12 bearing aircraft, carrying four ASCM each, escorted by perhaps twelve fighters and approaching from three points of the compass. Impossible to conceal, such a force would be detected and engaged initially by as many as twelve F-18 Super Hornets or F-35s in three flights of four at a range of three to five hundred nautical miles. With an historically empirical combat kill rate of 59% for the AIM-7

Sparrow missile and a compliment of four such missiles per

fighter (i.e., forty-eight Sparrows hitting twenty-nine plus

targets), it is possible for the first defenders to reduce this

force to seven or eight attackers able to reach their launch

point of 250 nautical miles.[81] If so, there would be some

thirty YJ-12 approaching the carrier from three angles.

Missiles launched from this range would provide the Aegis

system less than forty-five seconds to track and about thirty

seconds to destroy prior to the minimum range of the SM-3.

With a demonstrated kill rate against ASCM of over

90% in tests, the SM-3 missile would still require thirty-six

launches within this period, or one missile per second from

any of its networked platforms, to ensure destruction of these

missiles. As a Supercarrier task force might include four

destroyers and an Aegis cruiser, each with as many twenty-

four SM-3 missiles in vertically launched tubes, the supply of

[81] Barry D Watts. "Six Decades of Guided Munitions,"
http://www.dtic.mil/ndia/2006psa_winter_roundtable/watts.pdf
(accessed, 25 January 2016).

missiles is adequate, with even a single vessel capable of disgorging twenty-four such missiles in as many seconds. Assuming, however, that only one such vessel can engage, preferably the Aegis cruiser itself, these twenty-four missiles would leave as many as nine YJ-12 inbound to the carrier.

The *Nimitz* class CIWS consists of sixteen RIM-Sea Sparrow missiles in four quad launchers and four Phalanx Gatling guns. With an historic interception rate of 59%, and assuming all missiles were engaged, the Sea Sparrows would leave four or five YJ-12 for the Phalanx system to handle.[82] With a maximum effective rang of two nautical miles, these guns would have less than three seconds to engage the surviving missiles. Even should each gun engage and destroy one missile, one or two will likely penetrate: a theoretical penetration rate of 1.04%. Fractional compared to the kamikaze penetration rate of 23.11% during the Battle for Okinawa, but considerable given the mass production and deployment possibilities of unmanned missiles. With ever

[82] "U.S. Navy Sees Chinese HGV As Part of Wider Threat."

increasing range and speed, and with emerging AI and stealth, the Air Launch Cruise Missile remains an existential threat to the Supercarrier construct.

Modern Attack/Defense Scenario 3: Submarine/ASCM

Launch platform options for the YJ-12 include submarines, any one of which may launch up to six of the missiles at a time. In 2006, a Chinese *Song* class submarine surfaced within five nautical miles of the USS *Kitty Hawk*.[83] This was not the first incident where an American Supercarrier was surprised by a diesel-electric submarine. On August 10, 1998, during the RIMPAC '98 Exercises, the Australian diesel-electric submarine HMAS *Onslow* approached to within 300 yards of the USS Carl Vinson undetected, releasing flares to indicate its successful penetration of the carrier's defenses.[84] A year later, on

---

[83] "The Song Incident." February 6, 2007. http://fas.org/blogs/security/2007/02/post_2/ (accessed January 25, 2016).

February 1, 1999, during the JTFEX/TMDI99 Exercises

conducted with NATO vessels, the Dutch diesel-electric

submarine HNLMS *Walrus* theoretically "sank" the USS

Theodore Roosevelt along with several of her escort vessels.[85]

However, it is the *Song* incident that stands out due to the

potentially hostile intent of the subject nation.

Each *Song* class packs a six-tube battery that can

launch the YJ-12. The *Song* incident indicates that closure is

possible to a point with a maximum ASCM defense response

time of less than two minutes. As any *Song* crew willing to

conduct such an attack would be committing suicide

regardless of their success, it is fitting to use the above

demonstrated possibility as an example of a prospective attack

on a modern American Supercarrier in comparison to that of

the only previous experience of American carriers under fire -

WWII.

---

[84] Ibid.

[85] Ibid.

A single *Song* class submarine with six tubes loaded

with YJ-12 missiles would be able to launch six ASCM from

300 nautical miles out. Launches would likely occur at around

150 nautical miles range, half that of the missile, allowing for

thirty seconds for defenders to respond. Escort vessels

unaware of the existence of the submarine until that moment

would seek to both intercept the YJ-12 with the SM-3 and

destroy the launching submarine.[86] This means that eight or

more SM-3's would have to be fired within a twenty-second

engagement window to intercept the missiles. The carrier

itself would have three seconds to engage with little or no,

warning. Assuming the same defense as provided in the Air

Launch scenario above, it is likely that at least one of the

missiles would impact the vessel.

Given improvements in diesel-electric submarine

design in recent years, the Chinese saturation assault

[86] Richard Lehner. "Missile Defense Agency Responds to New York Times Article." May 18, 2010. http://www.dodlive.mil/index.php/2010/05/missile-defense-agency-responds-to-new-york-times-article/ (accessed January 24, 2016).

predilection, and the increased numbers of such vessels

capable of coordinating a multi-axis assault, the submarine

based ASCM, too, remains an existential threat to the

Supercarrier.

Modern Attack/Defense Scenario 4: Supercavitating Torpedo

Submarines have an additional threat capacity that

cannot be ignored giving both historical and recent events.

The super-cavitating torpedo is a high-speed underwater

device that creates a drag-reducing air bubble to facilitate its

passage, giving the weapon speeds as high as 200 kts. Range

of the Russian made Shkval 2 torpedo is just over nine

nautical miles. This gives a reaction time of less than two

minutes from launch detection to target impact.[87] Though the

current 460 lb. conventional warhead of the Shkval 2 is

unlikely to sink a Supercarrier (the 12,420-ton American built

---

[87] *Steven Ashley. (May 2001). "Warp Drive Underwater".*
http://www.scientificamerican.com/article/warp-drive-underwater/
(accessed January 24, 2016).

Brooklyn class Argentinean cruiser *General Belgrano*

required two British Mk-VIII torpedoes with 805 lb. warheads

to sink in the Falkland War), a lucky hit by one or a salvo of

four to six may render the vessel incapacitated long enough to

exploit any resulting tactical opportunity.[88]   The Shkval 2

also has a low yield nuclear option, which would mean sure

destruction of the target if employed.

A *Song* class armed with Shkval 2 type torpedoes that

has remained undetected at the range of the 2006 incident

would have surely (save for torpedo malfunction) scored at

least one out of six hits given that the target could only have

traversed 1,400 yards at 35 kts. Only one need be fired at all

in the case of a nuclear weapon. Given the relative dearth of

experience with anti-torpedo technology such as the Surface

Ship Torpedo Defense System and Countermeasure Anti-

Torpedo and the one-minute response time allotted at this

range, countermeasures other than maneuvering and alarms

would be minimal. It is probable that even a limited attack by

[88] Woodward and Robinson, 8-9.

one sub on a single axis would gain a hit, with the probability

increasing rapidly in a multi-sub, multi-axial attack. Too, the

Song class, or similar vessels of other nations, may be

rendered autonomous by drone technology and lay dormant

for extended periods at the sea bottom in wait of the specific

passive acoustic signal of the *Nimitz* or *Ford* class

Supercarriers.

Arguments that the *Kitty Hawk* and escorts were not

involved in anti-submarine warfare exercises at the time fail

to take into consideration the many lessons of Pearl Harbor,

among them being that conflict is not always considered

imminent when it arrives and that a nation rarely ends up

fighting the war it is prepared for. Post-World War Two

naval combat experience such as that of the Falkland War

indicate that large combat vessels can be sunk or heavily

damaged by modern cruise missiles and torpedoes even when

on a combat footing.[89] In the case of the HMS *Sheffield*, the

activated defensive systems including CIWS, Electronic

[89] *Woodward and* Robinson, *8.*

Counter Measures and chafe failed to prevent the impact of

one of two French made Exocet ASCM that had targeted the

ship despite early detection.[90] The proliferation and

advancement in technology of ASCM and torpedoes since

1982 and now (2018) has been quantum, with potential

adversary nations such as China, Russia, and Iran and North

Korea rather prudently researching means of engaging the

Supercarrier task force effectively – or at least mitigating their

efficacy. The *Forrestal* and *Enterprise* experiences of the late

1960s indicate that even light initial damage can result in the

incapacitation of exceptionally large vessels. Indeed, it is a

safe (if not particularly popular) argument that the

Supercarrier is quite vulnerable in the modern age.

Perhaps increased network capacity, possibly through

Artificial Intelligence, for enhanced CIWS, electromagnetic

shielding and increased early detection capacity for nascent

threats can provide continued survivability of the Supercarrier

in the emerging environment. This remains to be seen.

[90] Ibid.

Implications of Supercarrier Losses

7 Destruction of an American Aircraft Carrier, WWII (Public Domain).

The loss or incapacitation of a single American Supercarrier out of a limited fleet of ten, aside from the loss of a tenth of the naval fleet carrier force, would mean the loss of as many as 6,000 personnel. As noted by the *Hood* and *Bismarck/Tirpitz* historical examples earlier, such a loss would damage the national morale and limit the deployment options of the remaining Supercarriers – thereby diminishing their strategic and tactical value. In fact, the very existence of these emerging technologies has altered American naval warfare options.

During the Straits of Taiwan Incident of 1996, the

United Sates deployed two Carrier Task Forces centered on

Nimitz and *Independence* to support Taiwan, with the former

navigating the Straits as a show of force.[91] Given the capacity

of the DF-26/WU-14 ASBM and its difficulty in being

countered, such a carrier-centric "saber rattling" option may

no longer be viable in these circumstances. Such

advancements may also render the Black Sea, Sea of Japan,

and the Persian Gulf impassible to Supercarrier task forces in

times of potential conflict with Russia, North Korea, or Iran.

In fact, the mobile land based ASBM effectively renders the

South China Sea, Straits of Taiwan and most the Western

pacific a no-go zone for the carrier task force in a general

conflict with China. Chinese military theory and

technological aspirations indicate the probability of multi-

axial hypersonic ASBM and ASCM saturation assaults in

such circumstances, which, given China's regionally

numerical launch platform superiority in the Western Pacific,

[91] Chen Qimao. "The Taiwan Strait Crisis: Its Crux and Solutions". *Asian Survey* 36 (11). University of California Press: 1055–66.

compound the veracity of the Chinese A2/AD strategy for regional hegemony. Recent infrastructure developments in the South China Sea now provide Chinese military planners with additional strike launch options, though the more remote said bases are from the mainland the more acceptable they will likely be geo-politically to the White House and Pentagon as pre-emptive or retaliatory strike targets.

Missile bearing surface vessels and submarines would provide additional points of launch for such coordinated strikes, with the *Song* incident illustrating an extent capacity for surprise attack by submarine at extremely close ranges. Operating independently, submarines provide for a perpetual threat to the carrier group. In constricted water such as the Persian Gulf, et al, swarms of missile-bearing high speed boats could easily overwhelm the defenses of any naval combatant. Drone watercraft designed for stealth could deliver waterline blows to warships in such a scenario, with the U.S.S. *Cole* incident illustrating the damage that could be done by such explosive laden light watercraft.

The extraordinary monetary and resource investment in the Supercarrier, its lengthy time to construct and therefore replace and its increasing vulnerability in the emergent era collude to invoke these questions: Is the Supercarrier obsolete? What are the alternatives? Is it too late? The above analysis seems to indicate that the vulnerability of the Supercarrier should in fact be cause for concern and that other options should be studied.

Alternatives to the Supercarrier Concept

8 Rust never sleeps (Public Domain).

In retrospect, the investments in the costly battleship in the years leading to WWII would have been better spent on aircraft carriers, submarines, and destroyers, and generally in a more numerous, flexible, and survivable force that could not be so negatively affected by a single attack. Such a force could be in more places at once, providing concentration of force in time in well-coordinated attack or brought together at a focal point (potentially from many angles of approach) to concentrate force in space as well. This, of course, is a perspective forged in the foundry of after-though.

However, again through the auspice of hindsight, it is evident that an emotional attachment to battleships placed blinders on the advocates of the battleships and tainted their opinions on the emerging peril wrought by aircraft and submarines. There were also socioeconomic and political attachments as vote-seeking politicians whose constituents' jobs relied upon the production of the behemoths fought for their continued production. And there was of course national pride, which grand ships have garnered in countrymen since time immemorial. This paradigm still holds true today, with the Supercarrier assuming the role of the battleship in the hearts of adherents as the tides of technology, geopolitical and socioeconomic change and a sea of reality begins to rise about them. Nonetheless the inevitability of obsolescence must be measured and ultimately accepted. Alternatives to the Supercarrier construct must now be considered before the next Hampton Roads, Jutland, or Pearl Harbor.

Alternatives may include, as noted above, a more numerous and therefore more flexible and more survivable fleet of smaller carriers, perhaps thirty or more in the 50,000-ton *Forrestal* class range, each carrying fewer aircraft personnel, but employing more drones and Artificial Intelligence enhanced electronics and engagement systems potentiating overall operational efficacy.

The naval treaty limitation maneuverings of the Japanese and British in the early 1920s, intended to mitigate the United States' capacity to build many heavy cruisers instead of costly battleships in a truly short span indicates the historically accepted viability of the option.

Such a force, being capable of being in more places at once, would better fulfill the Mahan-inspired geostrategic naval-base theory of global hegemony adherent to American foreign policy. Additionally, the price tag for each of the new *Ford* class Supercarriers, at $9.4 billion, is three-five times of an Aegis cruiser, destroyer or attack or ballistic missile submarine. Discontinuing the Supercarrier would free funds for such alternative investments.[92]

Given the disperse sources of material necessary for the creation of this new Navy, new jobs and economic stimulation options also might be forthcoming in the process, as well as technological advancements stimulated during the redesign process.

Much like the carrier task forces of WWII, two or more such lesser carriers could operate together when necessary, providing redundancy to the task force aircraft in the case of individual loss, while also providing mutually supportive defensive firepower and offensive coordinated options. Such a force would be capable of both concentration of force in space and time. Current single-carrier task forces stand to be rendered tactically unviable with the loss of the solitary carrier, giving its aircraft nowhere to land as well, if remote enough from prepared land. Further, the fewer

[92] Congressional Budget Office. Options for the Navy's Future Fleet. (Washington D.C.: Government Printing Office, 2007), 19.

Supercarrier groups can only be in a few places at once, a

paradigm inconsistent with the emerging multi-conflict

environment.

Technologies developed for the *Ford* class

Supercarriers, such as electromagnetic catapults and increased

automation could be employed to enhance the combat

viability of the smaller carriers. Advancements in nuclear

propulsion systems may provide power for long-term

duration, while CIWS lasers and rail guns can provide point

defense without requiring recoil absorbing construction.

Laser cannon are currently being deployed upon lesser

naval vessels with their introduction to carrier point defense

inevitable.[93] These new defensive weapons, while currently

limited by certain atmospheric conditions, require no

ammunition, may be powered by the existing reactor system,

and produce no recoil, facilitating retrofitting to current

[93] "All Systems Go: Navy' Laser Weapon Ready for Summer
Deployment." July 4, 2014.
http://www.navy.mil/submit/display.asp?story_id=80172 (accessed
January 23, 2016).

vessels wherever space allows – in many cases supplemental to the existing CIWS. Further, developments in electromagnetic shielding, anti-torpedo-torpedoes and other defensive elements are emerging or forthcoming.

While these factors may increase the survivability of each of the new ships, the increased number of deployable ships available will increase the survivability of the fleet either when acting together or independently. Networking between warships and other situational assets will provide an umbrella of coordinated defensive systems such as is increasingly improving in the United States Navy today.

Lastly, one idea ripe for resurrection is the concept of "magazine ships." Converted fast cargo vessels (or possibly specially designed nuclear-powered ships) designed or modified to carrying hundreds of disparate missiles in Vertical Launch Tubes, networked to the Aegis system and on tap for any engagement personnel in the fleet to access. Such a vessel could also carry thousands of drones that can increase protection sorties to detect threats above and below the surface perpetually, more efficiently and at less cost than manned aircraft.

All these potential alternatives and/or technological advancements to the Supercarrier should be considered. Similarly, potential advancements in the existential threats to the Supercarrier must be considered. Only then can a rational decision about future funding be made.

Conclusions

9 Ford Class CVN (Public Domain).

The aircraft carrier's crucible of tactical validity

occurred in the Second World War, with no direct assaults

occurring against carriers since 1945. This seventy-five-year

period of theory-only development in defensive technologies

has never been tested in actual combat. Thus, the experience

of WWII is the sole source of empirical evidence to the

viability of carrier defense and the potentially existential

threat of saturation or asymmetric assault.

Through theoretical extrapolation of this practical evidence, no matter how temporally removed, prognostications with some pretense to veracity may be derived. To a large degree, both the offensive-threat and defensive systems of today are linear extrapolations of WWII technology. Anti-aircraft/anti-missile missiles, of which adequate real-world application data exists to interleave here, and electronic countermeasures, are among the few new paradigms extent in the carrier's defensive capacity.

In sum, military history is rife with examples of technology changing the status quo at sea. Through the annals of history, many a fleet has been swept away by the latest technological wave while their admirals clung in vain to the wreckage of their predilections and proclivities. So, it may be with the Supercarrier; so impressive, so ominous, so 'too big to fail.' The Supercarrier has been fundamental to American geostrategic hegemony for the last seventy-five years and a cornerstone of national pride. Yet hubris and nostalgia are poor foundations for military planning.

So, is the American Supercarrier still a viable means of projecting influence and military power in the emergent geo-strategic and technological environment? The answer is: Yes, for now, but maybe not for long. Alternative options must be explored before continued investment beyond the *Ford* class. And perhaps the Ford Class construction plan should be truncated with the eventuality of obsolescence approaching ever more rapidly.

Given the costs of modern weapons and the empirical costs of investing wrongly, rational, prescient decisions must be made. If objective analysis is executed and transformations warranted, the resulting opportunities must be embraced. The Imperial Japanese Navy embraced the last big change at Pearl Harbor. The People's Liberation Army Navy, the Russian and North Korean navies and the Iranian Republican Guard are embracing one now. The United States Navy, the foundational element of the United States' Mahan-inspired geostrategic policy, must stay one step ahead of any sea change to maintain their nation's global hegemony.

Bibliography

"Aegis Ballistic Missile Defense."
http://www.mda.mil/system/aegis_bmd.html (accessed January 22,
2016).

Aldrich, Richard. *Intelligence and the War against Japan.*
Cambridge: Cambridge University Press, 2000.

"All Systems Go: Navy' Laser Weapon Ready for Summer
Deployment." July 4, 2014.
http://www.navy.mil/submit/display.asp?story_id=80172 (accessed
January 23, 2016).

Arkin, Pringle and. *The Secret US Plan for Nuclear War.* New
York: W. W. Norton, 1983.

Ashley, Steven (May 2001). "Warp Drive Underwater".
http://www.scientificamerican.com/article/warp-drive-underwater/
(accessed January 24, 2016).

Beeton, Robert. *Naval and Military Memoreess of Great Britain,
from 1727 to 1783.* London: Shortman , Hurst, Rees and Orme,
1804.

Brands, Hal. *From Berlin to Baghdad: America's Search for
Purpose in the Post-Cold War Waorld.* Lexington: University of
Kentucky Press, 2008.

Bridgman, Leonard, ed. "The Grumman Hellcat." Jane's Fighting
    Aircraft of World War II London: Studio, 1946.

"Bunker Hill, CV-17." November 22, 2005.
    http://www.history.navy.mil/research/histories/ship-
    histories/danfs/b/bunker-hill-i.html (accessed January 11,
    2016).

Bulliet, Richard W., ed. *The Columbia History of the 20th Century.* New York: Columbia University Press, 1998.

Calvocoressi, Peter. *Total War: The Causes and Courses of the Second World War.* London: Peguin, 1989.

Campbell, John. Jutland: An Analysis of the Fighting. London: Lyon Press, 1998.

Clausen, Henry C. *Pearl Harbor: Final Judgement.* New York: Crown, 1992.

Congressional Budget Office. Options for the Navy's Future Fleet. Washington DC: Government Printing Office, 2007.

Coombes, Bill. "Divine Wind." The Commemorative Air Force Dispatch Online Archives, Spring 1995. http://rwebs.net/dispatch/output.asp?ArticleID=49 (accessed January 2, 2015).

Correll, John T. "Billy Mitchell and the Battleships", Air Force Magazine, June 2008, 64–67.

Diguilian, Tony. *21 September 2007.* *"United States of America: 5"/38 (12.7 cm) Mark 12"* *http://www.navweaps.com/Weapons/WNUS_5-38_mk12.htm (accessed January 3, 2015).*

"Document: China's Military Strategy." http://news.usni.org/2015/05/26/document-chinas-military-strategy (accessed January 25, 2015).

Dupuy, Trevor. *The Harper Encyclopedia of Military Biography.* Edison, NJ: Castle Books, 1992.

"Enterprise Remembers 1969 Fire." http://www.navy.mil/submit/display.asp?story_id=64783 (accessed January 25, 2016).

Evans, David, and Mark Peattie. *Kaigun: Strategy, tactics, and technology in the Imperial Japanese Navy, 1887–1941.* Annapolis, MD: Naval Institute Press, 1997.

Freidman, Norman. Naval Radars. Annapolis, MD: Naval Institute Press, 1981.

Friedman, Norman. *US Destroyers: An Illustrated Design History (Revised Edition).* Annapolis MD: Naval Institute Press, 2004.

Hoyt, Edwin P. *Pearl Harbor.* London: G. K. Hall, 2000.

Hoyt, Edwn P. *Japan's War.* New York: McGraw-Hil, 1986.

Jarecki, Eugene. *The American Way of War.* New York: Free Press, 2008.

Jones, Archer. *The Art of War in the Western World.* Chicago: University of Illinois Press, 1987.

Klemperer, Klemmens von. *German Resistance against Hitler: The Search for Aliies Abroad.* Oxford: Clarendon Press, 1992.

Lamb, Richard. *The Ghosts of Peace, 1935-1945.* Salsbury: Bloomsbury, 1987.

Lehner, Richard. "Missile Defense Agency Responds to New York Times Article." May 18, 2010. http://www.dodlive.mil/index.php/2010/05/missile-defense-agency-responds-to-new-york-times-article/ (accessed January 24, 2016).

MacNamara, Robert. *The Fog of War.* New York: Rowman & Littlefield Publishers, 2005.

Mahan, Alfred Thayer. "Armaments and Arbitration; Or the Place of Force in the International Relations of States." *Archive.org.* 1912.

https://archive.org/stream/cu31924007373560/cu31924007373560_
djvu.txt (accessed December 29, 2016).

——. "The Influence of Sea Power on History 1660-1783." *The Project Gutenberg.* September 26, 1890/2004. http://www.gutenberg.org/files/13529/13529-h/13529-h.htm (accessed November 17, 2016).

——. "The Interest of America in Sea Power, Present and Future." *The Project Gutenberg.* May 2, 1897/2005. http://www.gutenberg.org/files/15749/15749-h/15749-h.htm (accessed November 18, 2016).

Mee, Charles. *The End of Order: Versailles, 1919.* New York: Dutton, 1980.

Middlebrook, Martin and Patrick Mahoney. Battleship: The Sinking of the Prince of Wales and the Repulse. New York: Charles Scribner's Sons, 1979.

Millett, Allan R. and Peter Maslowski, William Feis. For the Common Defense. New York: Free Press, 2012.

Mitchell, Brigadier General William. "Strategical Aspect of the Pacific Problem" as quoted in Phillip Melinger, (Ed.), The Paths of Heaven: The Evolution of Air Power Theory. Maxwell AFB, Alabama, Air University Press, 1997.

Momiyama, Thomas S. "Supercarriers for Smart Super Power Diplomacy." *Naval War College Review* (Naval War College) 63, no. 3 (June 2010): 168-174.

Newhouse, John. *War and Peace in the Nuclear Age.* New york: Knoff, 1989.

"Operation Praying Mantis: A Look Back at How U.S. Naval Forces Responded to Hostile Forces in the Arabian Gulf." http://www.navy.mil/ah_online/ftrStory.asp?id=73470 (accessed January 25, 2015).

Paret, Peter. *The Makers of Modern Strategy from Machiavelli to the Nuclear Age.* Princeton, NJ: Princeton University Press, 1986.

Picknett, Lynn, Stephan Prior, and Clive Prince. *Friendly Fire: The Secret War Between the Allies.* Edinburgh: Mainstream, 2005.

Polmar, Norman. *The Naval Institute Guide to the Ships and Aircraft of the U.S. Fleet. Annapolis, Maryland: Naval Institute Press, 2004.*

Powaski, Ronald. *The March Toward Armageddon.* Oxford: Oxford University Press, 1987.

"Ship Force Levels." 1946. http://www.history.navy.mil/research/histories/ship-histories/us-ship-force-levels.html (accessed February 14, 2016).

Sowinski, Lawrence. *"The Essex Class Carriers," Warship Volume II. Annapolis, MD: Naval Institute Press, 2000.*

Stinnett, Robert. *Day of Deceit: The Truth about FDR and Pearl Harbor.* New York: Touchstone, 2001.

Sweetman, John. *Tirpitz: Hunting the Beast. Gloucestershire, England: Sutton Publishing Limited, 2004.*

Taylor, Bruce. *The Battlecruiser HMS Hood: An Illustrated Biography, 1916–1941. Annapolis, Maryland: Naval Institute Press, 2008.*

"The Battle of the Coral Sea," 2015. http://www.history.navy.mil/content/dam/nhhc/browse-by-topic/War%20and%20Conflict/The%20Battle%20of%20the%20Coral%20Sea/ww2-17.pdf (accessed January 2, 2015).

"The Battle of Midway." http://www.history.navy.mil/research/library/online-reading-room/title-list-alphabetically/m/midways-strategic-lessons.html (accessed January 2, 2015).

"The Halsey-Doolittle Raid," 2015.
http://www.history.navy.mil/research/library/online-reading-room/title-list-alphabetically/h/halsey-doolittle-raid.html (accessed January 2, 2015).

"The Kamikazes: Japanese Suicide Units." 2015.
http://www.history.navy.mil/content/dam/nhhc/browse-by-topic/commemorations/commemorations-toolkits/wwii/articles-on-world-war-ii-naval-aviation/pdf/ww2-31.pdf (accessed January 2, 2016).

"The Song Incident." February 6, 2007.
http://fas.org/blogs/security/2007/02/post_2/ (accessed January 25, 2016).

"The Washington Naval Conference, 1921–1922." *United States Department of State Office of the Historian.* 2014.
https://history.state.gov/milestones/1921-1936/naval-conference (accessed January 3, 2015).

"United States of America 20 mm/70 (0.79") Marks 2, 3 & 4."
December 2015.
http://www.navweaps.com/Weapons/WNUS_2cm-70_mk234.htm (accessed January 3, 2015).

"U.S. Carrier Task Force 58." 1992.
http://carl.army.mil/nafziger/944UFNA.pdf (accessed January 11, 2016).

"U.S. Navy Sees Chinese HGV as Part of Wider Threat."
http://aviationweek.com/awin/us-navy-sees-chinese-hgv-part-wider-threat (accessed January 23, 2016).

127

"USS Forrestal (CVA-59)."
http://www.navy.mil/navydata/nav_legacy.asp?id=64
(accessed January 25, 2016).

US Naval History and Heritage Command.
http://www.history.navy.mil/index.html (accessed December 8,
2013).

USHistory.org. *End of the Cold War.* 2014.
http://www.ushistory.org/us/59e.asp (accessed February 28, 2015).

Watt, Donald. *Succeeding the Bull: America in Britain's place - A
Study of the Anglo-American Relationship and World Politics in the
Context of British and American Policy Making in the Twentieth
Century.* Cambridge: Cambridge University Press, 1984.

Watts, Barry D. "Six Decades of Guided Munitions." 2017.
http://www.dtic.mil/ndia/2006psa_winter_roundtable/watts.
pdf (accessed, 25 January 2016).

Woodward, Sandy; Robinson, Patrick. *One Hundred Days: The
Memoirs of the Falklands Battle Group Commander.
(London: Naval Institute Press, 1997), 8.*

"World War Two Damage Reports and Photos" 2014.
http://www.paperlessarchives.com/wwii_naval_damage_re
ports.html (accessed January 3, 2015).

Qimao, Chen. 1996. "The Taiwan Strait Crisis: Its Crux and
Solutions." Asian Survey, 36 (11). University of California Press:
1055–66.

Zats, David. "Bofor Guns of World War II." 2001.
http://www.allpar.com/history/military/bofors.html
(accessed January 3, 2015).

Wyden, Peter. *Day One.* New York: Simon & Schuster, 1984.

Printed in Great Britain
by Amazon